FORM AND TECHNIQUE

"The Art and Psychology of Personal Training Sales"

An evidence based model in personal training sales

LaMarr Magnus, M.S.

authorHOUSE

AuthorHouse™
1663 Liberty Drive
Bloomington, IN 47403
www.authorhouse.com
Phone: 1 (800) 839-8640

© *2019 LaMarr Magnus, M.S. All rights reserved.*

No part of this book may be reproduced, stored in a retrieval system, or transmitted by any means without the written permission of the author.

Published by AuthorHouse 09/30/2019

ISBN: 978-1-7283-2112-7 (sc)
ISBN: 978-1-7283-2110-3 (hc)
ISBN: 978-1-7283-2111-0 (e)

Library of Congress Control Number: 2019910649

Print information available on the last page.

Any people depicted in stock imagery provided by Getty Images are models, and such images are being used for illustrative purposes only. Certain stock imagery © *Getty Images.*

This book is printed on acid-free paper.

Because of the dynamic nature of the Internet, any web addresses or links contained in this book may have changed since publication and may no longer be valid. The views expressed in this work are solely those of the author and do not necessarily reflect the views of the publisher, and the publisher hereby disclaims any responsibility for them.

CONTENTS

Introduction vii

Chapter 1	Prospecting 1	
Chapter 2	Initial Consultation / Confirmation Calls / Getting to Know Your Prospect 26	
Chapter 3	Initial Consultation / Fitness Analyses / Demo Workout 41	
Chapter 4	Price Presentation 66	
Chapter 5	Overcoming Objections 80	
Chapter 6	Client Renewals 101	

Acknowledgments 111

Bibliography 113

INTRODUCTION
A NECESSARY CLIMATE CHANGE

The purpose of this book is to introduce to the exercise science student and fitness professional the art and psychological aspects of selling high-quality fitness programs to anyone. This text will provide a foundation and systematic approach for the mastering of the art of the sales process to the exercise science student and fitness professional alike through various behavioral, psychological research studies and practical experience. After studying and practicing the tools within this book, fitness professionals will be more *efficient*, *sharp*, and *accurate* when it comes to building value and presenting their training programs. Fitness professionals will also have more *self-confidence*, *conviction*, *credence*, and *faith* to grow their business in a professional and skillful manner.

With over twelve years of fitness management experience and a master's degree in human performance, I have had the chance to teach and educate fitness professionals the vast majority of the psychological skills needed to become successful. There needs to be a climate change in the way we look at presenting personal fitness programs. When I came into the fitness industry about twelve years ago, it was all about the sale and the bottom line. I've had managers and vice presidents call me relentlessly during shifts, pressuring me to make someone just sign the bottom line. And there it was: the dawn of fitness sales. Was this personal training? I thought I was going to be helping people. I have a four-year degree, and it led to this: getting hammered to sell, not administer goals and build rapport ... just sell.

After a while of not getting any sales and no clientele, I began to get discouraged by the arena of personal training. During my master's degree program, I began studying more about the psychology of human behavior, which led to various research studies and papers in motivation and behavioral psychology. I began to apply those tools with my staff of trainers and colleagues, which led to tremendous success and many managerial promotions. After being one of the few personal training managers to sustain my management position (after six months, most get fired or just quit), constantly hit sales quotas, being durable, and learning the process, I started putting the puzzle together on how to make this process of selling high-quality fitness programs more prestigious. Over the last twelve years, I've learned the dos and don'ts, techniques that work, and the ones that don't. I've witnessed fitness professionals succeed and fail. After being in fitness management for so long, I knew that I wanted a different outlook with my staff and the way we approached our fitness programming.

The climate of fitness programming is watered down and artificial, and it creates a platform of unethical behaviors and discouragement. Many gym goers have had a bad taste left in their mouths from personal trainers who are pushy, salesy, and fabricated. The attrition in personal fitness programs and fitness professionals is at an all-time high. A recent report from IHRSA shows that only 5 percent of clubs have an attrition rate less than 30 percent.[2] Most fitness clubs in America have a rate between 30 and 50 percent, meaning that every year the fitness industry loses up to 50 percent of its members. Another research study, performed by the Fitness Industry Association in 2001, shows the typical six-month

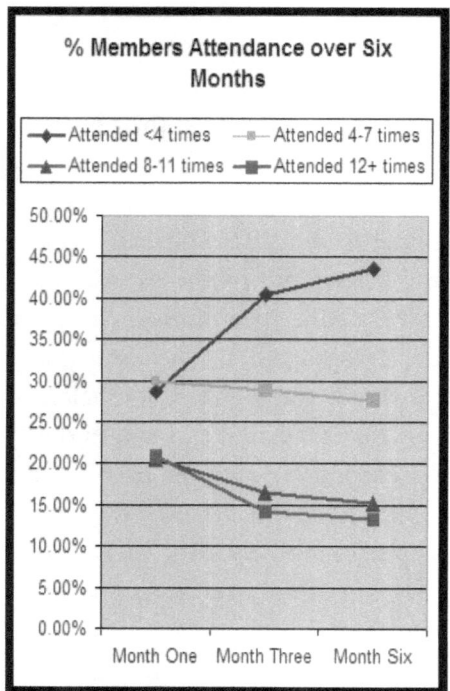

tenure of a gym member.[1] From the research, we gather that attendance generally decreases over time. Attendance reduces dramatically if attendance started out low in the first month. The difference between attendance in months three and six is minimal, suggesting that attendance patterns are well established by month three.[2]

At month six, around 29 percent of members use the club eight or more times a month; typically we would classify this as active membership.[2] At month six, around 27 percent of members use the club between four and seven times a month; typically we would classify this as low usage membership. Usage and retention go hand in hand; the more members use the facility, the more likely they will stay. There needs to be a war on fitness attrition!

We combat attrition by increasing usage; we increase usage by getting members results, which come from fitness professionals. But wait, there is a constant rotation and revolving door in the field of fitness, and why? Too hard? Not enough money? Not enough clients? Yes, yes, and yes, because most fitness professionals aren't prepared mentally for the risk, the stage, the rejection, the assessing, the rapport building, and the emotional roller coaster that is involved with being a successful fitness professional. Unfortunately, most psychological tools effective in building value in fitness programs aren't shared in most accrediting bodies, universities, and fitness clubs. I can testify myself to observing trainers wheeling and dealing trainer packages like used cars salesmen. I have also frequently seen potential clients just handed a pricing sheet without a full presentation. Those behaviors lead to fitness programs and professionals lacking credibility and performing unethical transactions that devalue the platform of fitness.

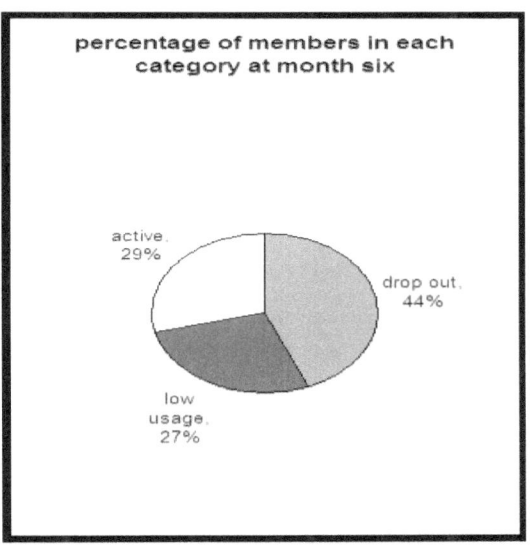

A study done by the *Industrial Marketing Management Journal* in 1993 named "Shortcomings of Sales Programs" explained that more emphasis is being placed on sales training programs because companies want to better equip their salespeople with new or improved job skills.[10] The investigation also stated that more attention must be placed on sales training and having specific objectives set and used to plan training programs, evaluate success, and assess needs.[10] A systematic approach to sales training will provide the skill, knowledge, and attitude for success. The fitness industry should follow suit and provide a similar format. Fitness professionals and students entering the world of professional fitness should be educated on certain psychological skills and strategies to build better value in presenting their programs in a high-quality fashion. Standards need to be elevated. A panel discussion called "Trainer Attrition, What's Wrong" at the Brookbush Institute of Movement Science reported that in order to gain more long-term fitness professionals and fight attrition, the field must be made more prestigious.[3] One of the panelists mentioned a marketing education sector of fitness and credentials like DPT would give more prestige to the profession.[3]

Form and Technique presents a standardized professional method of presenting fitness programs that will lead to greater retention of loyal clientele, greater confidence in the sales process, and an increase in closing percent. All fitness professionals, whether yoga instructors, strength coaches, or personal trainers and students of exercise science alike will learn the psychology of *building value and presenting* fitness programs professionally and efficiently. *Form and Technique* will change the landscape of the fitness profession by providing a manual that brings incredible value and a standardization of selling personal fitness programs based on psychological, behavioral, and social science research. This will ultimately lead to further retention of fitness programs and higher quality of presenting fitness.

This manual will make the actions of the fitness professional easier, like carrying a load down a hill. The strategies and techniques used within the text all come from research in the areas of behavioral, social, and personal psychology. There are phrases to memorize verbatim, called tie downs-for example, and mind-sets that must be practiced in order for the method to work. Some of the other psychological learning objectives behind *Form and Technique* are effective framing, positioning, theory of emotion, and motivation. Engaging with various personality types and how to influence and motivate are also important within *Form and Technique*. No matter the environment, whether it is a gym, park, or recreation center, and no matter the particular specialty of the fitness professional, this book will give psychological strategic methods to build value in fitness programming and gain new clientele. Like anything in life, if you want to be great, you must practice. Given the time and effort of your practice of the methods, you will be able to demonstrate your value as a fitness professional within a few minutes of meeting anyone who is even thinking about working with a professional or even if they're not thinking of working with one. Fitness professionals are selling a number of things: *motivation*, *energy*, and a *belief* that if done right, results will occur.

The passion behind my writing this book lies in the aspect of increasing the quality in the field of fitness and seeing more successful fitness professionals influence behavior positively. Too many fitness professionals begin in the field and then get discouraged due to the fact that they weren't equipped and taught certain psychological tools to assist. So instead, fitness professionals will find shortcuts to build their business or create negative habits that will lead to shortfalls in their career. This creates a cheap and distorted image of the art form that we love. The future of fitness is to be a landscape of quality certified fitness professionals influencing and changing lives efficiently and with intention, without the bitterness of artificial programs, poor influences, and attrition of clientele. With each relationship gained, some could last a lifetime, and the information you teach will last a lifetime as well. As fitness professionals, it is our right to hold the profession with dignity and class. Presenting yourself and the program you offer will be the single most important factor in your value and success as a fitness professional.

As a training director over the last twelve years, I have over ten years of influencing thinking in regard to fitness. I have sat through hundreds of sales meetings and countless business seminars, and they all have taught me something different that I have used in part of my success today. My goal is to reach every person who is interested in the fitness profession and share with them standards that will increase their level of confidence and career as a fitness professional from a psychological viewpoint in presenting fitness programs.

Over the last twelve years of selling PT packages, I have developed and lectured on the quality of presenting fitness programs. Most of the methods found within *Form and Technique* originate from behavioral, personal, and social psychological research applied more toward the fitness professional. I have had tremendous success teaching form and technique to managers and over one hundred fifty trainers within the last five years. Success of teaching form and technique has led to my site reaching company records in recognized revenue. Within one year of my methods being applied, revenue profits doubled. Over two years, profits tripled, and the number of sessions redeemed reached a grand total of sixteen hundred, which is equal to nearly $150,000 in revenue per month; my direct supervisors were very happy with such a tremendous growth rate. Personally, I have sold over $700,000 dollars in training contracts over the last ten years. Once I stepped down from the managerial role into just a trainer role, I received the record for the most clientele within the first three months in my company. I signed up forty clients within the first three months and generated over $50,000 in sales revenue within the first three months. My peers were fascinated by the way I was able to grab someone off the treadmill, and next thing you knew, they were a paying client. But remember, I wasn't a trainer who'd just gotten his certification; I had been mastering and developing my approach over the last ten years. So finally the company saw my strength and gave me a position to teach sales training to the new hires, which is fun because it gives me the opportunity to do what I love, teaching.

This book is being written because I want to share all the methods and strategies that I have developed, learned, and mastered over the last twelve years. I want this book to be implemented into the exercise science curriculum and every fitness professional library right next to their books of exercise physiology because the sales aspect is a key tool to learn and standards need to be elevated in order to be profitable and successful fitness professionals. This text will discuss the psychological aspect to every component of the sale. From prospecting to assuming the sale to the actual closing technique being used, the new trainer will be comfortable and confident in attempting to recruit and prospect a client. These tools and strategies weren't shared with me in school, and all exercise science students and fitness professionals need these strategies to be successful and gain new PT clientele. The climate of fitness needs a major upgrade in the way we present and view programs. *Form and Technique* will teach, motivate, and inspire the fitness professional to master your craft and build high-quality programs with loyal clientele.

Mission Statement:

After studying and practicing the tools within this book, the fitness professional will be more efficient, sharp, *and* accurate *when it comes to building value and presenting their training programs. The fitness professional will have more* self-confidence, conviction, credence, *and* faith *to grow their business in a professional and skillful manner no matter the environment or fitness niche.*

CHAPTER 1

PROSPECTING

Objectives

Understanding and mastering

- mental tools of prospecting
- psychological principles for prospecting
- personalities
- methods/tools for prospecting
- prospecting verbatim

Prospecting

1. Activities designed to search for potential customers/clients[1]
2. Possibility of something happening soon: a chance or the likelihood that something will happen in the near future, especially something desirable
3. Vision of the future: something that is expected or certain to happen in the future or a mental picture of this

If fitness professionals don't have anyone in front of them to offer the service to, then the career will become daunting and boring very quickly. Many fitness professionals fail in the act of converting leads to loyal clients, a challenge that will lead a fitness professional to either downfall or *success*. The jump start of any fitness professional's career begins with building relationships, marketing services, and transitioning potential leads to loyal, permanent clients.

The fitness professional must have and practice certain psychological mind-sets in order to readily prepare for the prospecting journey of meeting anyone and everyone in the environment. The successful fitness professional will carve out time to master psychological strategies that we will cover in this chapter. Becoming a master of the art of marketing and selling is a key indicator to how your business will jump-start and take off. Like athletes mastering certain biomechanics of a sport, musicians practicing their instruments, and actors rehearsing their lines, fitness professionals must practice their art. It is crucial for fitness professionals to practice the process of marketing and selling their service. Whether you work at a small, local gym setting, university gym, or downtown, big-box gym, everyone around you is a lead. If you're at a park or other setting, more questioning may be needed to find out why a person is there. Everyone needs your *help*; keep that in your mind! Everyone in a gym or working out is looking for something; whether they want to be in shape, relieve stress, gain more mass, become quicker, jump higher, or gain weight—everyone is there for something. These individuals are considered *leads*. Prospecting is a skill that may come easily to some and be difficult for others. The process of prospecting must be mastered to build success, and rejection is a dynamic in prospecting that the fitness professional must become seasoned to. There are two main reasons to prospect:

FORM AND TECHNIQUE

1. To demonstrate a service for an individual based on his or her goals or to set up an appointment to conduct a demonstration workout or consultation
2. To gain a new client based on analyses of workout and education and build value based on how your services can assist

In order to be a successful trainer, you will need to give many demonstration workouts to future clientele. They must taste before they buy. Once again, prospecting is the hardest part of the selling process because it requires the most patience and mental fortitude to keep going at it. Practice it, and it will become second nature.

Mental Tools and Physical State of Prospecting

The fitness professional needs a sharp and focused mind-set to prospect. Prospecting requires a sense of confidence and positivity. An upright posture and a high chest deliver a message of strong character. People need to know you're in the room, so eye contact is necessary. Tone of voice and correct questions will make prospecting a comfortable experience, and yet certain individuals will shun your approach—don't worry, and keep swinging.

Preparing yourself mentally is also key when prospecting. Adjust your mind to meet a certain number of people per day, and further hold yourself accountable for reaching a certain number. This accountability and discipline will only lead to future success. Be prepared for rejections while prospecting; know that it is coming. Remember, the goal of prospecting is to influence individuals to share their time with you to give you an opportunity to showcase your value as a trainer.

A fitness professional who doesn't make prospecting second nature will struggle to keep their business afloat. I have had countless meetings with fitness professionals about how prospecting and keeping their lead generation pipelines wide open are vital to their businesses due to attrition. When fitness professionals do not prospect, they are basically saying that their businesses are *closed* and no new business is welcome. Being physically and mentally prepared will add to the chances of high-percentage prospecting and lead generation. Here are some psychological principles to prospecting and influencing behavior that will lead to high value and greater lead generation:

The principle of *liking* tells us it's easier for people to say yes to us when they know and like us. Fitness professionals must practice the element of *liking*. There are many things we'll say yes to when a friend asks. On the flip side, we're usually quite comfortable saying no to someone we don't know or don't like. For example, if a friend asked you to go out for dinner after work, it would probably be easy to say yes. But if someone you don't know asks, I bet it would be just as easy to say, "No, thanks."[4] It will also be easier to coach someone who will say yes to your advice if they know and like you.[5] One way to master this powerful psychological tool is to search for commonalities with the prospect and give genuine compliments.[6] Whether a person likes a basketball team, shares the same interest in shoes, or comes from the same town as you, finding something that you have in common is vital to creating an immediate connection. It's not about them liking you; it's about them knowing that you like them. As the old saying goes, people don't care about how much you know until they know how much you care.

A clear illustration of the principle of liking is how the Tupperware Brands Corporation uses it.[7] The request for purchase of the product doesn't come from a salesperson; it comes from a friend to every person in the room, usually a neighbor who has invited friends over for a product demonstration in an environment where everyone knows each other. The company organizes goods to be sold by a friend rather than an unknown salesperson without any rapport.

Similarity can also increase liking, according to research completed in 1970 on peace marchers.[8] Subjects were more likely to sign a petition with a requester similarly dressed to them and would even do so without reading the petition.[9] Having a similar attitude and values is of major importance when getting a prospect to like you. Car salesmen are trained to look at the background of a person trading in a car.[10]

The power of praise can be a great psychological tool to increase liking. Evidence comes from Cialdini's principle of persuasion.[11] A 1978 study by Drachman, de Carufel, and Insko, in which men received personal comments from someone who needed a favor from them, illustrates the principle. Some men received only positive comments, some received only negative comments, and some got a mixture of good and bad. The conclusion was that the person who gave the positive comments was liked the best. Another finding was that the praise didn't have to be accurate; compliments work even when they aren't true.[12] When beginning to prospect and build rapport with prospects, remember that if they like you, they will be more willing to take advice and comply with suggestions that you have for them.

The principle of *consensus* tells us that when people are unsure how to act in certain situations, they tend to look to others to see how they should respond. It makes me think about the old saying "There's safety in numbers."[13]

First, share with people whose behavior you're trying to change. Share information and stories about your success with people who have made a decision to change already. Examples: "This new workout routine has an 80 percent success rate for body fat percentage lost and muscle gain." "Eight out of ten members have seen improvements with yoga added to their cardio routine two times a week."

Second, share the exact actions of what successful people are doing.[14] Example: "Research shows that doing HIIT training twice a week will cut body fat by 45 percent."

People feel more comfortable when they know there have been many other satisfied customers.[15] Project satisfaction as you extend your service. Elaborate on how past customers were satisfied or how results were achieved. Fitness professionals can always rely on past testimonies and success stories when meeting someone new. Sharing a past success story of old clients will increase your credibility by using the principle of consensus to build value and achieve greater influence.

The principle of *reciprocity* is another psychological tool that can be used to gain leads and build quality value in service. The reciprocity principle states: *One should be more willing to comply with a request to the extent that the compliance constitutes reciprocation of behavior.*[16] People will return a favor with a larger favor. As a fitness professional, you are going to have to *give* to *get*. Offer a glimpse of your service; give a sneak peek into your value. Usually people will give back something in return, and usually the return is more valuable—like committing to a fitness program. Companies and organizations use this principle all the time: give a quick gift, and then ask for a donation. Extermination companies offer free home inspections; these companies rely on the premise that once they give you the information to influence your thinking, you will not delay with a decision and will also be motivated to return the favor of the free inspection.[16] Tip jars are always filled with some dollars to give the perception that previous tips were given. The fitness professional should always be willing to give gifts, invite, educate, demonstrate, and give favors, knowing that by virtue of the norm of reciprocation, a prospect will feel obliged to repay in the future a favor or gift that was given. Offering your service as a fitness professional is like giving a taste test of a fine wine.

The principle of *authority* is a vital psychological tool that can be used by a fitness professional to gain influence and build leads through prospecting. If you are a person of authority, you are extremely influential.9 In the early stages of life, it is your parents and teachers who are the people of authority. Later it's police officers, and yes, your trainer!

People will comply with the wishes of an authoritative figure as is illustrated in a study conducted by Bickman and published in 1974. A requester wearing a security guard uniform received more compliance (pick up a bag, stand on the other side of the street) that was irrelevant to the security guard's domain authority. (Bickman 1974) As fitness professionals, we are experts, and people will comply when references and citations are indicated during dialogue. Examples of how to use the authority principle follow.

"Mrs. Jones, it was a pleasure meeting you last week. You told me that you want to get back in shape and strengthen your lower back. Did you know that the Journal of Health and Science recently reported that active stretching will lead to low back injuries? Do you have five minutes for me to show you some stretches?"

"Excuse me, sir. Do you mind if I share something with you in regard to your back squat? A new article from the Strength and Conditioning Journal showed that having a neutral spine during your back squat will lead to greater range of motion around the lumbo pelvic hip complex. Do you have five minutes so I can show you?"

"Excuse me, sir. Are you trying to get big (hypertrophy) or get lean? Okay, cool! The National Academy of Sports Medicine suggests that a moderate tempo and longer rest periods will lead to greater gains in strength. Do you have five minutes so I can show you?"

Many people want shortcuts, so what do they do? They run to the experts. As a fitness professional, embrace the fact that you are an expert with superior knowledge and most people will comply with a request or suggestion from an expert. Having cited quotations and statistics readily available will also increase your level of credibility. Having the confidence to state from an authoritative standpoint suggestions and tips at first may be intimidating. But a little practice goes a long way. Find a niche or a criterion that you want to specialize in in regard to fitness and then read, read, and learn about it. Practice it relentlessly, and naturally what will occur is a gain in confidence and authoritative demeanor when discussing that particular topic.

Dionte, an Old Soul with New Authority

I am reminded of a trainer whom I hired by the name of Dionte Russell. Forty-six-year-old Dionte was the old soul of our training team as he was the eldest in age. Most of his training style derived from the old school—fundamental dumbbell movements; that's all he knew. I mean, trust me, this guy was built like a Mr. Olympia and had incredible strength for his age, so I wasn't doubting his credibility in any way, shape, or form. His business was beginning to decline, and I wanted nothing but the best for him and his business so I challenged him to gain a stretching certification to create a more dynamic service that he could offer to members. I wanted his brand of service to have more value. I had to open his eyes to various areas of fitness that would make his business more profitable. I had a conversation with Dionte, and he agreed with me wholeheartedly and accepted the challenge. Immediately after we had this conversation, Dionte injured his Achilles tendon and was unable to work for five months. In that time Dionte was still committed to the challenge; he would text me and email me the books he was reading to create a stronger brand of business for himself. Month after month Dionte read and learned, taking three certifications in various areas of dynamic warm-up and active stretching. Dionte returned to work as the new authority in the area of posture, balance, and active stretching. He would advertise, promote, and just give free demos to individuals around the stretch area. Dionte saw tremendous growth in his training business after he began to initiate conversations with individuals about his authoritative stance in stretching and postural assessments. The dumbbells were down, and stretch mats were out. He reshaped his business by adding and becoming an authoritative figure. Whether it is stretching, boxing, Pilates, Zumba, or yoga, become the authoritative figure to provide suggestions and influence behavior.

The principle of *scarcity* is another tool widely used by fitness professionals. "Learn twenty yoga poses in one hour, and burn over five hundred calories! Only eight spots left!" Sound like something you've heard before? The principle of scarcity states that if opportunities and the items they contain seem more scarce, then they are perceived as more valuable.[6] What is less available is considered more valuable. It is a fundamental relationship between supply and worth, as stated in Cialdini's principle of persuasion.[5] Fitness professionals can use this tool by offering a service and mentioning that there are a "limited" number of spots, so sign up now. As fitness professionals, we can influence prospects to perceive that an item is scarce and increase the immediate worth of the item, whether it is a yoga conditioning class, movement screening, or lean body mass test.

A research study conducted by Worchel, Lee, and Adowal proved that cookies were more desirable and attractive to consumers when they were scarce rather than abundant.[11] They proved that scarcity can affect value. In addition to physical items, items of information can hold a scarcity value as well. Here is an example for the fitness professional using the principle of scarcity to generate leads:

<u>Learn the five Pilates secrets to a lean waist and sculpted lower body.</u>
1 day only
7 spots left …

Limited access to information and opportunity will lead to people wanting that information and opportunity. Fitness professionals should practice the art and psychology of scarcity, which will add value to services being offered. The principles and tools stated above can be used in a multitude of situations and environments by fitness professionals.

The principle of *urgency* can be used by fitness professionals as much as scarcity. A classic study by Howard Leventhal analyzed the effects of handing out tetanus brochures to subjects. Leventhal conducted the study by handing out two different pamphlets, both sparing no detail on the horrid effects that the tetanus disease can have on the body.[20] The first pamphlet described only the effects of tetanus, while the second included information on where to get vaccinated. Those who had the second pamphlet (with the sparse follow-up info) were much more likely to take-action; the rate that followed through with vaccination was superior to the first group by nearly 25 percent. As fitness professionals, we must identify and issue or acknowledge a concern and create an action plan by giving specific instructions on what to do next.[20] Inform your prospects about the concern and drive them toward specific actions. For example: *"Mrs. Jones, right now your BF is 34 percent, which is a little high ... Would you like to learn more ways on how to get that number down? Let's meet tomorrow, and I will show you some fitness ideas/tips that will get that number down immediately. Let's set up a time for tomorrow—is evening or afternoon better for you?"*

Understanding Personalities: Who Am I Training?

Fitness professionals will increase their success by building rapport, so let's look further into rapport building and take a look at the psychology of personality traits. The fitness professional can easily direct, influence, and motivate a prospect if he or she has a vivid understanding of that person's personality traits. Most fitness professionals aren't aware of the psychosocial game being played while getting to know someone. This idea bring me back to a consultation I completed with a woman who was in her midthirties, overweight, and very closed and reserved. How was I to break the ice with her? Her face was of stone, and when I probed her with questioning, her replies were short and concise. I knew that in order for me to become her trainer, she needed to like me, and I was failing miserably within the entire hour. Finally it hit me: during the entire hour, I'd never asked about why she was there; I was just talking and assuming everything. So I asked her, *"Mrs. Jones, why are you here today?"* She looked me in the eyes and said, *"I feel unpretty."* She was discouraged about getting back on the dating scene after a major breakup. Boom, there it was; I knew her why. I knew her mental state, and I knew her reasoning for being there in that moment with a fitness professional. Her personality was filled with the pain of feeling unsatisfied and devalued by the way she looked.

So with that said, I took that bit of information, nurtured it, and wove it into the entire consultation from the program design of her workout to her baseline measurements. I empowered her with the belief that she could do anything she put her mind to. The psychological tool of imagery allowed her to envision herself with a new body, more fit, dating, smiling, and having fun. I constantly throughout the entire consultation was tying down what she was doing to how she was going to *feel* about herself. Those tools allowed me to influence her within sixty minutes to start a twelve-month, three-times-a-week program with a value of over $10,000. That is one of the prime examples of how a fitness professional can have leverage in influence if they have a complete awareness of a person's personality traits.

Mccrae and Costa concluded that there are five major traits that serve as building blocks for personality.[13] The chart below shows the five traits and how to manage them.

Openness: Individuals with a high level of openness have a general appreciation for unusual ideas and art. They are usually imaginative, rather than practical. Being creative, open to new and different ideas, and in touch with their feelings are all characteristics of these people.[13]

How to Manage: Provide them with information and material for them to learn; talk about advancing their program and taking their fitness to a new level, trying new modes of exercise, new tempos; allow them to be creative with programming and goal setting.

Conscientiousness: Conscientiousness is about how a person controls, regulates, and directs their impulses. Individuals with a high level of conscientiousness on a career test are good at formulating long-range goals, organizing and planning routes to these goals, and working consistently to achieve them despite short-term obstacles they may encounter. Other people usually perceive a conscientious personality type as a responsible and reliable person.[13]

How to Manage: Set specific goals, set achievement goals, set rankings and daily or weekly plans for them to follow, email instructions, set calendar dates, give homework.

Extroversion/Introversion: Extroversion indicates how outgoing and social a person is. A person who scores high in extroversion on a personality test is the life of the party. They enjoy being with people and participating in social gatherings and are full of energy. A person low in extroversion is less outgoing and is more comfortable working by himself.[13] On the other side of the coin are introverts. These people have less exuberance and energy than extravorts. They are less involved in social activities and tend to be quiet and keep to themselves. An introvert does not require the external stimulation that extroverts do.[13]

How to Manage: With extroverts, become a friend, a trusted advisor; act in social arenas, stay excited, match their energy, mirror, give them attention, and make them the center of attention with their achievements. With introverts, use imagery to elicit emotional responses, give them homework to complete by themselves, have more private conversation and be less social with them. Give time for them to think, hold virtual conversations, reward their efforts, and give time for them to speak.

Agreeableness: A person with a high level of agreeableness in a personality test is usually warm, friendly, and tactful. They generally have an optimistic view of human nature and get along well with others.[13] Agreeable prospects find it important to get along with others. They are willing to put aside their interests for other people. These individuals are helpful, friendly, considerate, and generous. Their basic belief is that people are usually decent, honest, and trustworthy.

How to Manage: Set goals based on research standards and rankings. Become a friend and develop trust. Give them extra-credit assignments that coincide with their fitness program. Ask them to cooperate in certain tasks or events that will lead to a trusted relationship. their Increase self-efficacy by acknowledging their ability and achievements.

Neuroticism: Emotional stability refers to a person's ability to remain stable and balanced. At the other end of the scale, a person who is high in neuroticism has a tendency to easily experience negative emotions. These are people who say, "I can't," and always put negative words in their speech. On the flip side, someone who is low on neuroticism is usually emotionally stable and calm and does not constantly experience negative feelings. Prospects who are high on neuroticism are very emotionally reactive. They will have an emotional response to stress or have many bad moods.

How to Manage: Ensure they are not in anxiety-filled situations and have no pressure; help them feel confident by building a language; exercise improves their mood (through positive chemicals); deep breathing and relaxation strategies help them cope; be positive and use motivating language.

Methods of Prospecting

The goals of these various prospecting activities are to build rapport, invite, inform, educate, and correct, ultimately leading to a scheduled appointment on how to correct an assessment given or to provide a demonstration of service. The American Council on Exercise terms building rapport as a "relationship marked by mutual understanding and trust," which is one of the foundations in the ACE IFT model.[12] "Building rapport is a critical component of successful client-trainer relationships, as this process promotes open communication, develops trust, and fosters the client's desire to participate in an exercise program" (ACE Personal Trainer Manual, p. 84). It begins with saying, "Hi." The prospecting activities may vary depending on the fitness professional's environment. Prospecting activities should be divided in order to have different activities done every day. The successful fitness professional will use most of the activities and switch up on a daily or weekly basis. Do not just fall to being good in only one area; try to master them all. The experienced and successful fitness professional can reinvent themselves and adapt to generate leads no matter the environment.

Walking the Floor *(Authority/Liking Principle)*

This involves approaching members of a gym, recreation center, free weight area, cardio area, or the street. It is a bit intimidating at first, but once a role is assumed, the behavior will become second nature. Wherever you decide to reach out to future clientele, that is your floor of leads. Who are you looking to speak to? As the gym "expert," you're looking for anyone who has incorrect form, is susceptible to injury, has a look of confusion, or anyone deserving of a friendly fitness tip. The goal is to build rapport, invite, inform, educate, and correct.

Think of yourself as the gym concierge, the "helper," the "spotter," the "towel guy," or the gym "specialist." The secret to walking the floor is to look and act busy, with casual conversation that leads to information being shared. Another role to assume while walking the floor if you're inside of a fitness center is quality control. This involves acting as if you are the director of operations and having dialogue with members about the equipment operation, equipment layout, or temperature of the gym, casually engaging with the member. You can also undertake the "busy trainer" role, for example, the workout is complete, and all you need is someone to test it out to gauge the difficulty. Busy trainers are valuable trainers. If you approach someone and you offer a test run on the difficulty of a workout, it shows that you have confidence in them, and if they choose to do it, they believe and have confidence in themselves as well. Walking the floor requires a little self-assurance and assertiveness, but after a while, it is basically all about starting conversations that are valuable, influential, and trustworthy.

FMS (Functional Movement Screening) *(Authority/Consensus)*

The functional movement screen is a movement assessment tool used to evaluate compensatory movement patterns. Inefficient movement strategies may reinforce poor biomechanical movement patterns during typical activities, resulting in injury.[14]

To complete an FMS assessment, rank and score the prospects, and ask what they are doing currently to assist with issues. Invite them in to assist with current imbalances and how to start a program to correct imbalance within a movement pattern.

Static Postural Assessments *(Authority/Consensus/Urgency)*

This assessment can be done anywhere. It is used to identify any postural deviations, which may lead to tight or inhibited muscles.[15] This assessment examines the way a client looks while assuming a relaxed, standing posture. Specifically, observe the ankles and hips in the frontal plane (adduction), hips in the sagittal plane (anterior or posterior pelvic tilts), and the shoulder, thoracic spine, and head positions in several planes.[15] A more detailed description can be found on the ACE website. As mentioned before, once an assessment is concluded, begin to have dialogue about an invitation to learn exercises/modalities that assist with current imbalances and how to start a weekly program to correct imbalance within a movement pattern.

Lean Body Mass Test *(Urgency/Authority)*

This is to determine an individual's total lean muscle in pounds by taking the BIA test and entering calculations to determine lean body mass. Further explain how to gain lean body mass, and ask appropriate/interview questions. Invite the individual in for a demo workout on program design for muscle gain. This is a great tool for all populations; everyone is concerned about lean mass and fat mass. So let's educate, invite, question, and build rapport. This is one of the best conversation starters for a reserved fitness professional or a social butterfly. This test creates a platform for the authority principle to be used at its best, by educating about fat-burning activities, fat-burning intensities, nutrition, exercises—you name it, and a conversation can be started about either muscle mass or fat mass. Be the authoritative figure and educate to influence.

Demo Workouts *(Reciprocity/Urgency)*

This involves demonstrating a new exercise or set of exercises to individuals who want to attempt to work a certain area ... the taste test. The principle of reciprocity can be applied to this lead generator. Give, give, give, and then you will get. This is great for generating leads with individuals who are open to new ideas and programs and also for the fitness professional looking busy. Wherever you are, people are watching you. Your demo workout is your time to be onstage. This is your tryout for the main show; the show is to provide value in working with a trained professional enough for the prospect to hire you. Attention to detail and making it fun are essential for the workout to be challenging and specific. Provide a quality service, don't forget to assess and share concerns, and most importantly, invite the individual in for another demo workout. Keep in mind the demo workout is truly a demo; do not show the whole bag of marbles. In other words, if a full training session includes warm-up,

FORM AND TECHNIQUE

cooldown, and active stretching, take out a few things that might make the session "full."

Strength/Cardio/Agility/Pilates/Yoga Assessments
(Authority/Consensus)

These assessments all require you to determine an individual's measurement or rank on the following modes of fitness. Upper body or lower body strength by using various standardized tests, for example, push-ups, sit-ups, and wall sits. A one-mile run or step test to determine cardiovascular endurance. A T-test or shuttle run to determine agility. Pilates and yoga assessments can be organically made based on the discipline of the professional. For example, for yoga, how long can they hold warriors or a chair? Can the prospect complete a full vinyasa flow? Check joint stability on the knees, hips, and ankles. Pilates moves can be used for assessment purposes like yoga poses as well. The most important factor is to rank the prospect among others healthy or fit individuals, maybe set a soft goal (imagery), and invite them to learn more on how to increase performance. Most individuals will seek out exactly what parameters of fitness they are excelling at or weak at. Providing a professional gauge with industry-accredited standards for individuals is a great way to start conversations and build relationships with individuals in the fitness world. Once tests are complete, whether it is yoga or a boxing demo, go over concerns and invite the individual for another assessment or provide options for them to begin a program.

Email/Administrative

This is a method of inviting a certain crowd of people or individuals to a demo workout, seminar, workshop, monthly fitness newsletter, or social media page. This method can be a great mode for generating leads. Create a Facebook page or your own articles on fitness. Answer questions that many people may have. Provide tips and educate, educate, educate, and remember to cite all sources for credibility. Conduct thirty-, sixty-, and ninety-day follow-ups. You must pound the emails and phones if you are not a floorwalker or social butterfly. The email/phone call must be precise, welcoming, and straight to the point. I've had my share of trainers who weren't the best at approaching people on the floor, so what you do is you acknowledge and nurture their other gifts. There is also the gift of operational administrative work. Create and design emails for every type of client, whether a new member or one at a thirty-, sixty-, or ninety-day follow-up. Have a phone script specified for different types of populations that you will be reaching out to.

All of these skills can be practiced and learned. Keep in mind that a true fitness professional will be well-rounded in both the administrative platform and the actual walking around engaging with individuals' platforms as well. It is your choice to practice both and learn both, which will lead to future success of the fitness professional. Take the time to invest in and master your craft. To truly grow your fitness business, carve out time to do the administrative duties listed above, which will ensure that you will develop the skills needed to constantly look for new leads. Your business will not thrive if attrition occurs due to the lack of administrative prospecting.

Blog/Newsletter/Social Media

Blogs can be used for many reasons by the fitness professional to build a quality business. They can help drive traffic and gain useful leads. Blogging is a great way to establish a repository of content. Blogs are public posts, usually about a topic or area of discussion of a problem that most people have. Writing a blog can assist with establishing authority and gaining trust, especially in the fitness industry. An article on blog.hubspot illustrated that businesses that use blogs gain 67 percent more leads.[16] Blogs are a great tool for many fitness professionals, especially if they are not social butterflies when it comes down to prospecting and generating leads. Blogs are free and very cost-effective. All you need is a little time and some material, and you're on your way. Fitness professionals can also brand themselves by creating an insightful blog. I have had trainers use blogs to start conversations, to debunk fitness myths, and also just to give tips and suggestions. Social media is another great tool to use to bring attention to your brand.

This brings us to the story of Austin, a twenty-two-year-old trainer from a small town in Texas. He was just walking through downtown

Chicago and stopped by the gym where I was the fitness director. He came through the door and began to have a look of awe at how big the gym was. He wasn't used to the size and the numbers of people; it was his first time in a big city. One thing he did have, however, was a strong spirit and mental fortitude that was unmatched. He was filled with pure determination. He wanted the job badly; he wanted to really impress his family back home and prove that he could make it in the big city. With that said, of course I believed in my ability to teach, and I just needed the right pupil. He was experienced in theater, so the skill of presenting and building value was pretty natural for him. Austin was also eager to learn every step of the sales process. Austin took notes and recorded all of our meetings. He was a true student of fitness and firmly believed in every tip and psychological strategy I taught him. Every member he met, he wrote down their email and asked for them to join his email group on Facebook. He was relentless at building his business through social media. He wasn't the best at floor walking, and even his workouts weren't magical, but his drive for notoriety and passion for helping is what separated him from the other eighteen trainers on staff. Austin had Facebook posts, Instagram notifications for his sessions, and live feeds for his boot camp classes. And he was barely in the gym. After six months of hard work and diligently improving his social media business, Austin had over three hundred followers. He added over forty new clients to his business. He was well over $12,000 in recognized revenue every month. He excelled and grew his business with his own efforts and the tools of social media. He is currently one of the top trainers and group exercise instructors in Chicago.

Standards of Prospecting

The fitness professional who wants to be successful at prospecting must have a set goal in mind to achieve. The fitness professional must be motivated to strive for that goal. An article by Frank Smoll (a sports psychologist at the University of Washington), "ABC's of Goal Setting," explained that goals should be specific, positive, and both short-and long-term in order for the goal to increase motivation.[17] Having a daily or weekly number to reach will always give you direction and a sense of accomplishment. The goal of prospecting is to invite individuals and showcase your value as a trainer that will enable you to assist them with getting to their goals. A fitness professional must become accustomed to never giving up and becoming numb to "no" in his mental state. Not everyone you talk to and offer your service to will just simply smile and say "yes." Don't take any rejection personally; rejection is a common activity that occurs to a fitness professional. Most of the time, a "no" isn't a no; it's a "not right now." Knowing the numbers and probabilities behind rejection is also wise when analyzing success at prospecting. One out of every four people talked to usually will be interested in your service and show up for a demonstration if there is impactful dialogue. So there is a 25 percent chance of gaining a new lead. Once you get the lead to show, that will be considered a showed appointment. And of course, the final step is to build enough value for the prospect to hire you. So if we take that small sample of one out of four with the usual 50 percent closing percentage and scale it to reach a total of two clients, we need to talk to a total of sixteen individuals. Sixteen individuals will lead to four shows (25 percent), which will lead to two clients. That's an average of a 25 percent show percentage and a 50 percent closing percentage. That is the usual probability that I tell all fitness professionals when they begin to prospect. By no means am I a math connoisseur, but a fitness professional must have a grip on probability and know the chances taken aren't unwarranted or a waste. Prospecting is a numbers game and involves building the value of your service in a short matter of time to as many individuals as it takes to get to your goal, whatever the goal may be. Creating a forecast for yourself will keep you accountable to your prospecting and growth of your business.

Setting up an alternate appointment date for a prospect to participate in your service is the final outcome when prospecting. Not every situation and result with prospects will be the same; it is crucial to learn from each prospecting situation and gain clarity from it. There will be mistakes made. A study at the University of Southern California explained the human brain learns in two ways—either through avoidance learning, which trains the brain to avoid committing a mistake, or through reward-based learning, a reinforcing process that occurs when someone gets the right answer. Scientists have found that making a mistake can feel rewarding, though, if the brain is given the opportunity to learn from its mistakes and assess its options.[18] The study showed that in certain circumstances, when we get enough information to contextualize the choices, our brains will essentially reach toward the reinforcement mechanism (positive feeling), instead of turning to the avoidance mechanism. With that said, our brains are going to assist us in the skill of prospecting by giving us signals and brain stimulation to repeat success and becoming more skillful based on the mistakes we make.[18]

Keep in mind that every prospecting situation will be organic if time is available; a demonstration at that moment may be an outcome as well. In an average eight-hour workday, one must collect up to twenty to thirty leads. That's four to six new leads per hour. Successful fitness professionals will attack prospecting, create a forecast for themselves, set a goal, and make a mistake, planning to learn from it.

Building Value during Prospecting and Verbatim Dialogue

What is said during prospecting sessions is crucial. Are you making an *impact*, or are you just talking gibberish? The purpose during the prospecting is to establish yourself as credible, understand every prospect's situation through questioning, and uncover a broader and deeper range of information for strategic objectives. Now remember, the goal is to invite the individual in for another demonstration workout or analyses of fitness goals. What you say and how you say it will determine your overall success. Many fitness professionals have no clue what to say, which can lead to a generic and watered-down perception of a fitness professional.

Open vs. Closed Questions

The fitness professional should be able to control conversations when beginning to prospect. One way to control conversations and not let the aim of the conversation go astray is to ask probing questions. Knowing the timing for asking open-ended and closed-ended questions will be a vital part of the prospecting journey and getting prospects to converse with you. It will take a little practice, but eventually it will become second nature.

Open-Ended Questions: Although any question can receive a long answer, open-ended questions deliberately seek longer answers and are the opposite of closed-ended questions.[25] When fitness professionals want meaningful and thoughtful dialogue, they choose open-ended questions.

They ask the respondent to *think* and reflect. The respondent will then give *opinions* and *feelings*. The fitness professional hands control of the conversation to the *respondent*.[25] When the fitness professional has time in the initial consultation, open-ended questions are ideal for building rapport and meaningful conversation.

Open-Ended Examples for the Fitness Professional

- How long have you been a member here?
- Why is working out important?
- What's keeping you motivated to work out?
- You're looking down; is everything okay?
- You're sweating pretty hard; what are you training for?

Closed-Ended Questions: A closed-ended question can be answered with a single word or phrase. Most of the time, respondents give you facts. Closed-ended questions are easy to answer. Respondents are quick to answer. Closed-ended questions set the prospect up for the desired positive and negative frame of mind. They keep control of the conversation with the fitness professional. Closed-ended questioning is great for prospecting because it allows the fitness professional to test the understanding of the prospect and then opens a window to build value, which is a crucial part of influencing and establishing credibility.

Closed-Ended Examples for the Fitness Professional

- What are you working on next? Arms/back?
- So you want to gain size, more of the back or chest?
- Are you happy with your current results?
- If I could wave my magic wand, what three areas would you want to work on the most?
- If I could show you a new way to activate your abs in less time, would you let me?
- Would you like for me to show you a variation of that lunge?

Listed below are a few icebreaker open/closed-ended questions to start conversations with individuals, whether inside of a gym or outside. You must listen and pay close attention to what is answered, so you can follow up with the proper answer or question. You must uncover their internal reason for being there. Some people are willing to express their reasons for being there, and some people are more hesitant. Remember, as fitness professionals, we are experts and the leading authority when it comes to exercise program design. Here are some example phrases to use and questions to ask when prospecting.

What are your goals? (-pen-ended)

Prospects must be specific when answering; get as specific a reply as you can. Getting prospects to talk about themselves is essential when asking this question. It is a must for them to share what body parts and areas they you are most interested in. When asking this question, try not to leave it open-ended; give options for them. For example: What are your goals: toning, sculpting, building endurance, losing weight, gaining muscle, relieving stress? Eighty percent of the time, they will give you an answer for you to work with. Once they answer, you have the option of either asking another question or inviting them for a demonstration for you to show them how to work on the area they described to you a moment before. If they are not available now, which is optimal, then set an appointment up.

Great job on the push-ups. Do you mind if I show you a new hand position for a stronger bench? (Action Paralysis)

If the fitness professional sees an exercise that may cause injury or potential harm, or on the other side of the spectrum, if a fitness professional sees an opportunity to advance a prospect, this is a great example of how to convey an impactful message with minimal parameters. Offering your expertise on a specific limb movement or technique of an exercise can be a great way to build trust and credibility and add value for your services. A research study at Arizona State University showed that a slight variation in wording in door-to-door donation requests can affect the total number of donations received.[19] Here are the example statements used in the study.

Quote #1: Would you be willing to help by donating?

Quote #2: Would you be willing to help by giving a donation? Every penny will help.

People who were asked the second variation were twice as likely to donate. The study showed people are more likely to take action when minimal parameters are set. Implying that small actions can lead to big results will make people more motivated to donate. Eighty percent of the time when a fitness professional asks the question to assist or show something new and original with minimal parameters, most people will say *yes*. Once they commit to learning from you, it is your job to keep the momentum flowing by giving impactful suggestions and offering the prospect to visit you again for more education, tips, suggestions, and so on.

What are doing next after what you're completing now ... arms, back, abs?

They must be specific with this answer. Getting them to describe the next part of their workout is key. Most people working out have no clue on program design. They usually have just read something in a magazine and are trying to replicate it. This is an actual quiz question also to test their knowledge of fitness in regard to their exercise program. Remember, everyone in the gym is there for a reason. Do not leave the question open-ended. For example, ask: What are you working on next ... arms, legs, abs? Eighty percent of the time, they will answer "maybe abs" or something to that effect; that gives you the opportunity to invite them for a demo or ask another question, like what exercise are they going to do? Opportunity arises to verbalize to them about your strengths as a trainer and how you can show them a few exercises for that area or that goal. This is a key opportunity to invite them for a workout at that moment as well.

How long have you been working out here? (Liking)

This question gives you the opportunity to teach or invite prospects for initial analyses if they are new or to demonstrate something new if they are old. Either way, this is a great conversation starter. Commonality is key with this question because no matter the answer, you can create a dialogue with the prospect.

I see that you're doing some nice crunches. Are you trying to get defined abs or just maintaining a strong core? (Action Paralysis)

This type of question will elicit the incorrect variables being used by the prospect during their workout. You challenge the prospect by classifying and acknowledging what the focus of the workout is and what type of workout they are completing. You give options just in case they cannot classify what their focus is. In this case, the options are (1) to get defined abs, and (2) maintaining a strong core. As certified professionals, we know the differences in terms of intensity, rep count, and rest period if someone is building muscle and if someone is working on stability (which is more rehab focused). Once an answer is given, continue to be positive and offer a solution, tip, alternate exercise, or maybe a demo workout, with a minimal set of parameters. As experts, we have a good idea of the vast differences in variables depending on clients' goals. As fitness professionals, politely asking what their focus is and offering a tip, suggestion, or demo workout will be a great way to educate and generate leads no matter the environment.

Most of these phrases, will lead the prospect to a response that can open the door for you to give advice, teach, demonstrate, and educate. All you need is an opportunity to give. Give and show you're an expert with confidence and pride.

Closing Prospect on the Next or Initial Appointment/Getting a Commitment

Closing the prospect or influencing a new prospect to meet another time with you is the next important step in gaining initial commitment. Once you have asked enough questions and either completed a demo workout or any other form of prospecting, there are four points to cover with the prospect.

1. Get the goal of what the prospect wants; have a true understanding of their mission.

2. Have results either from tests or a demo workout. For example, poor muscle percent, body fat percent, push-ups, and so on.

    Example: "Mrs. Jones, great job on the demo workout today. You have great leg strength, but I would definitely want to work on your spinal mobility (struggled with (insert concern) in the workout, and upper body strength due to (insert concern/imbalance here). Besides that, you did a great job. I would love to invite you in for another demo session a little longer and more focused. Are you available on Friday?"

3. Set a new short-term goal for the prospect and then invite them on a demo workout with you based on concerns you have with the prospect's performance.

    Example: "Mrs. Jones, you did a wonderful job on the planks. In a few weeks, I would love to see you hold for two minutes straight. Trust me; we will get there."

4. Set up another date for a demo workout or request a form of contact, whether it is email or a phone number. Remember to inform the client of the time length of the next appointment, usually sixty minutes.

Covering all four points is a must, and it must be practiced. It will come naturally for some and be difficult for some. During this practice, there will be rejection, but remember: it's a numbers game. The more shots you take, the more likely you are to hit.

Prospecting starts with saying "Hi," getting to know people, and building as many relationships as you can. Reinvent yourself, be bold, have confidence, be corporate, or be a social butterfly. Certain psychological mind-sets must be applied in order for the prospecting journey to be a success. Once you have someone in your hands, *impact, influence, educate,* and *invite* them in for another demo. Once a prospect commits to your service, act as if they are your client already and just *assume.* Think the activities through; the more participation, the better. Divide your prospecting activities into different daily or weekly activities.

Example Prospecting Day

Monday Eight-Hour Shift

6:00 a.m.–6:30 a.m. Walking the floor (free weights)—assisting with form/technique/cuing

6:30 a.m.–7:00 a.m. Walking the floor (stretch area)—assisting members with stretching technique

7:00 a.m.–8:00 a.m. Abs demo workout (ten-minute quick and easy)/ten-minute yoga/Pilates demo

9:00 a.m.–11:00 a.m. Workout/ Emails/Phone Calls—thirty-, sixty-, and ninety-day follow-ups

11:00 a.m.–12:00 p.m. Walking the floor (machine area)—assisting with form/technique/cuing

12:00 p.m.–2:00 p.m. Body fat % testing/lean body mass testing

2:00 p.m.–3:00 p.m. Emails/Phone Calls—thirty-, sixty-, and ninety-day follow-ups

3:00 p.m.–5:00 p.m. *Break*

5:00 p.m.–6:00 p.m. Ten-to fifteen-minute demo workout (abs/yoga core routine/Pilates core routine/kickboxing)

Key Points to Remember When Prospecting

- Mentally prepare yourself to prospect: act as if you own the place, meet everyone. It's a numbers game.
- Use and practice all psychological principles.
- Know your personalities.
- Know the eight ways of prospecting; practice and master all of them.
- Build value through proper questions.
- Always request another time to meet by gaining a form of contact.

Exercise for Prospecting

Walk to any busy grocery store. Introduce yourself professionally and hand out tips for working out, just for an hour or two. This exercise will get you and your mind used to talking to total strangers with confidence about a subject area that you're an expert in. Some people will want to talk, and some *won't. Practice.*

CHAPTER 2

INITIAL CONSULTATION / CONFIRMATION CALLS / GETTING TO KNOW YOUR PROSPECT

Objectives

Understanding and mastering

- appointment confirmations
- relationship and rapport building

- SIFM and the investigation stage
- example questions

The initial consultation, whether prospects were met in a fitness environment (gym, park, recreation center) or as part of a first member experience, this is the first time the prospect has committed to meet with you. They have psychologically contemplated, prepared, and taken action according to the transtheoretical model of behavior change.[24] You have influenced and motivated them to invest time with you. This is your opportunity as a fitness professional to show your value. It is your job to get the prospect to commit and maintain a program with your services. Set yourself apart from the rest. Create/build a relationship and set expectations. Get to know who this prospect is. Being able to identify what type of personality is in front of you and building rapport will take a little time, but practice is the key. Create comfort for all parties.

This initial meeting is important because this is when you have the chance to uncover the prospect's true emotional reason for wanting to change. Why do they want to work out? This is the opportunity to dig, dig, and probe with confidence. To fact find. As a fitness professional, the opportunity to perform fitness analyses or a demonstration workout to identify strengths and weaknesses of the human body will be your ultimate worth as the most tangible piece of evidence for warranting your service. All of these psychological parameters within the fitness consultation will need to be accomplished and mastered. At the end of this initial consultation, enough value should have been built to show a program and conduct a price presentation.

Confirmation of the Appointment

Once the appointment is set from prospecting activity, the prospect must be contacted immediately, either through email, phone, or whatever avenue they gave you to use. Confirmations show true professionalism; all the top companies in the world provide confirmations of appointments one to two days before the actual appointment. A quality confirmation call will support and build a relationship between the client and fitness professional. I have found in my professional experience that the fitness professional who commits to making confirmation calls feels more confident in their next day's business and has a greater show percent of appointments overall. As a fitness director for so many years, you have heard time and time again about fitness professionals setting an early morning/late evening appointment a week in advance, coming in for the appointment, and the prospect or client not showing up. From the customer standpoint, here are some benefits for confirming.

- Confirmation reminds the prospect/client of the appointment, thus making sure he/she will be there, and establishes the length of the meeting.
- Confirmation provides a better understanding of what will happen on the call and sets expectations for both the prospect/client and the salesperson.
- Confirmation gives the prospect/client the opportunity to talk with the salesperson before he/she arrives on the appointment, helping establish some rapport before the actual meeting.
- Lastly, confirmation allows the prospect/client to ask any questions he/she may have before the appointment.

Prospects must be contacted or reached out to to confirm their next appointment to ensure commitment is still there. A study by Patient Prefer Adherence 2016; 10: 479–499 (21) showed how health-care services are increasingly utilizing reminder systems to manage negative effects. The study explored the effectiveness of reminder systems for promoting attendance, cancellations, and rescheduling of appointments across all health-care settings. The study showed that in the absence of clear contraindications, all health services should use simple reminders for all patients. There was consistent evidence that reminder systems improve appointment attendance across a range of health-care settings and patient population subgroups.[21] More intensive reminder alternatives may be relevant for key groups of patients: deprived, ethnic, substance abusers, and those with comorbidities and illness. There is evidence that reminders can be used to optimize appointment and reminder systems. Health services should tailor reminder systems and adopt supportive administrative processes to enhance attendance, cancellation, rescheduling, and reallocation of appointments to other patients.[21]

Another study, by the Department of Pediatric Dentistry, found that confirmation reminder phone calls made even one day or two days before will elicit a reduction in the percentage of broken appointments in a pediatric dental clinic.[22] Patients were randomly assigned to three groups: (1) confirmation call made one working day before appointment, (2) confirmation call made two working days before appointment, and (3) control group (no confirmation call). Clinic staff made confirmation calls during normal office hours. Patient arrival was classified as (1) less than or equal to fifteen minutes late, (2) greater than fifteen minutes late, or (3) broken appointment. A confirmation call resulted in 93 percent of patients keeping their appointment as compared to 63 percent in the control group ($P<0.001$). If the health-care field has made confirmation calls a part of their procedures for patients to show up for medical appointments, then the fitness professional should abide by the same rules.

There are four strategies to focus on to assure prospects show up to the next appointment from a confirmation call.

1. Repeat short-term goals within the confirmation, if they were obtained during prospecting.
2. Repeat the x-factor if obtained during prospecting activity or ask for a goal.
3. Repeat something specific or personable about the client if obtained during prospecting activity.
4. Give specific directions/tasks to complete before attending the next appointment.

These strategies in the confirmation process are necessary to assure that the prospect will show up for the initial appointment. If an individual is unable to communicate the four main areas to focus on in a single call, then I would recommend a script to assist. The script will ensure that nothing is left out and will create a smoothly executed call. The confirmation call will provide the prospect with the value of being listened to and know what they were saying is important to you. The initial confirmation call will be a great window and opportunity to begin building value with your future client. Paying close attention to what a prospect is saying is a skill that must be mastered as well. As stated earlier, cancellations and no-shows will occur, but the more you practice confirming appointments, the easier it will be to increase the value in the appointment.

Example Phone Confirmation Script

Hello, Mrs. Jones. This is John, the Pilates instructor from the health club. We met last week … How are you doing today? (Take notes.)

It was a pleasure meeting you last week. You sounded really enthused about gaining more core and pelvic strength so you can bowl more. (x-factor)

How did you feel after our little five-minute demo? (Take notes.)

Great!

Were you able to cook up that baked broccoli that you were talking about having that evening? (Be personable.)

How did it turn out?

Okay great. I have you all set for our first Pilates appointment on Wednesday the twenty-third at 5:30 p.m. It will be a little more intense than last week, but fun! If anything changes, please shoot me an email or even a text. I look forward to working with you.

In addition to the phone call confirmation, email confirmations are a great way to remind the prospect of an appointment. Email doesn't intrude on the prospect like a phone call. When sending an email, always remember to be clear, be specific, and don't make it too long.[23] I usually have a formal email and an informal email to use. The informal email will have more of a personal touch in the email, restating something specific or their x-factor.

Example Email Confirmation (Formal)

RE: Shawn Williams—Appointment Confirmation

Dear Clinton,

This is a special reminder to confirm your fitness assessment/demo workout with Shawn Williams tomorrow, June 18, at 10:00 a.m.

Your meeting is scheduled to be held at Premier Health Facility on the ground floor at Lanceman Street, Mainland China. The place is accessible by cabs.

This is Shawn's cell phone number, just in case: +18157479837.

Please feel free to contact me if you have any questions. I would be happy to give any necessary assistance.

Thank you and have a great meeting.
Best Regards,
LaMarr Magnus, B.S., M.S.
Master Trainer
lmagnus@trainer.com

Example Email Confirmation (Informal)

RE: LaMarr—Yoga Strength Time

Dear Christy,

It was a pleasure meeting you yesterday. And great job with the yoga strength demo! We spoke briefly about learning some yoga strength routines that will increase your core strength and overall leg strength as well. I have you set for Monday at 8:00 a.m. You can meet me at the activities desk by the top of the stairs. It will be awesome!

Please feel free to contact me if you have any questions.
LaMarr Magnus, B.S., M.S.
Master Trainer
lmagnus@trainer.com

All in all, a confirmation or reminder of an appointment is essential to the fitness professional in many ways. I have hammered in my years of educating trainers the importance of the confirmation call. Especially when people are beginning this behavior change, they will need added accountability to assure that the behavior is staying in line with the goals agreed to. Value can be built with a confirmation call; trust, accountability, and most importantly rapport are created when a confirmation call is made. Set yourself apart as a fitness professional and make it a crucial part of your business to confirm all appointments.

Getting to Know Your Prospect / Relationship Building

Once a prospect has decided to commit to your appointment, the first half of the sale is complete. You have influenced them to take time out of their schedule to meet with you. They see a value in meeting with you. Now the prospect must maintain the belief that you can and will assist them in whatever their fitness goal may be. Taking immediate ownership of their issue is crucial in the sales process. *People don't care about how much you know, until they know how much you care.* Building a long-term relationship and having a permanent client is the goal. Building a relationship and getting to know your prospect is literal. *Dialogue and discourse remain the foundations of effective human communication,* whether in marriage, friendship, learning, or business. The open, respectful exchange of ideas around a shared interest or a common purpose and the willingness to listen, learn, and share with others are powerful glue for the fitness professional. Knowing prospects' personal behaviors, such as spending habits and how often they eat out, will assist with your program design and selection of programs. Uncovering the prospect's internal reason for wanting to change is another main reason for knowing why they are there. This is a very important step in the consultation appointment. Having all this information at your side also gives you hard evidence on why a behavioral change is required if future objections arise.

This is the time of the appointment when you begin to probe and fact find to gain as much information as possible so it can be used as reference for later when building value in their exercise program and starting their fitness program. Remember the purpose of probing (open-ended) is to get to the bottom of things. Your prospects want a good listening to, not a good talking to! They don't want to just sit there listening to your monologue of why your services are the best. A prospect wants to know that you understand their situation in detail.

These questions are intended to dig deeper than the surface. This is the window of opportunity to flood the prospect with questions specifically to fact find and gain greater insight into who this prospect is. As mentioned in the previous chapter, these open-ended questions will lead to answers that need to be thought about and will allow for feelings and opinions to be shared. Taking notes during this time will be useful to record all answers and ideas shared during this interviewing portion of the appointment. An acronym used during initial consultation to ensure that all the personal information is obtained is SIFM. All fitness professionals should go through these distinct personal areas to cover all aspects of the prospect's personal life in the beginning of the consultation to gain a vivid picture of where the prospect is in relation to starting a program.

Rapport Building

Rapport is the sense of connection you get when you meet someone you like and trust. It is a bond that forms when you discover that you share one another's values and priorities in life.[48] According to the 1990 study of Linda Tickle-Degnen and Robert Rosenthal, which appeared in *Psychological Inquiry*, the nature of rapport in terms of a dynamic structure has three interrelating components: mutual attentiveness, positivity, and coordination. In early interactions, positivity and attentiveness are more heavily weighted than coordination, whereas in later interactions, coordination and attentiveness are the more heavily weighted components. These components are summarized below.

- **Mutual attentiveness**: You're both focused on, and interested in, what the other person is saying or doing.
- **Positivity**: You're both friendly and happy, and you show care and concern for one another.
- **Coordination**: You both feel in sync with one another, so that you share a common understanding. Your energy levels, tone, and body language are also similar.

Many rookie fitness professionals struggle with this aspect of the appointment because they simply haven't lived enough life to touch base and build a strong connection with an individual. Most fitness professionals are so concentrated on working prospects out that they aren't mindful of this profound step in the appointment/sales process. The fitness professional must take time to understand and become fully aware of who is in front of them by *building rapport*. Here are some basics to rapport building.

- Smile.
- Be kind.
- Remember names.
- Listen attentively.
- Find commonality.

Commonality is big when encountering a prospect who isn't totally outgoing or is introverted. Polish anthropologist Bronisław Malinowski was the first person to study small talk, back in 1923.[48] He described it as "purposeless expressions of preference or aversion, accounts of irrelevant happenings, [and] comments on what is perfectly obvious." In other words, speaking for the sake of being sociable, rather than to communicate information.[48] Small talk is a skill that all fitness professionals must learn, especially when attempting to build rapport. Search for commonality. "Nice shoes; where did you get them from?" is an example of searching for commonality. "Do you like the White Sox or Cubs?" is another example of commonality searching. Show a genuine interest in *them*. Once again, *people don't care how much you know, until they know how much you care.* Use open-ended questions to discover who the person is and share experiences ... traveled to the same state, you both hate traffic, you both like X-Men movies, and so on. Search for commonalities. This will allow the prospect to open up and establish a line of trust. People love talking about themselves, so this is the time to show interest in them as a person.

A study completed in the Department of Psychology at Harvard University by Diana I. Tamir and Jason P. Mitchell showed that humans devote 30 to 40 percent of speech output solely to informing others of their own subjective experiences.[49] Individuals place high subjective value on opportunities to communicate their thoughts and feelings to others, and doing so engages neural and cognitive mechanisms associated with reward.[49] In other words, it is rewarding when people have the opportunity to talk about themselves, so let them talk!

Storytelling

As a seasoned fitness professional, I've learned that the art of storytelling is a great way to build rapport, capture attention, and live vicariously through someone else's experience. According to Kristi Hedges, an executive leadership coach at Forbes, telling stories will accelerate the interpersonal connections between two people.[28] Most stories can change and alter the way people think and act. A Stanford research study showed that statistics alone have a retention rate of 5 to 10 percent, but when coupled with anecdotes, the retention rate rises to 65 to 70 percent.[27] As a fitness professional, having success stories or examples of past clients will bring a sense of reality to the new prospect in front of you. One tip to assist with storytelling is to keep a log of a few good stories from past clients.[27] Another tip with storytelling is to have a story ready when you're about to stress a certain point. It gives more resonance and substance to the information given.[27] All in all, storytelling is a great way to build rapport and give real, credible examples of experiences that help send a message.

Uncle Larry, the Rapport King

Larry Mcdowell is a fitness professional with over fifteen years experience as an elite trainer in Chicago. I have had the pleasure of working with him over the last seven years, and he has exhibited that this portion of "getting to know your prospect" in the consultation can make the biggest impact for the sales process. Larry's retention rate is undoubtedly most impressive, to say the least. He has clients whom he has been training for nearly twelve years. Larry is a master at getting prospects to open up. His psychological skill of becoming *liked* was one I had never seen before. He had the ability to sit with a client, and within twenty minutes, you would think that they were best friends for twenty years. Larry would slowly and deliberately ask questions that would get the prospect to open up. Larry also had an interesting way of letting prospects know how much he cared by sharing stories of family and past clients that would hit home with most of his prospects. That was the effect he had on his clients. There was instant trust, instant rapport, and of course, an instant sale! Larry's goal in mind was to fully know his client as much as he could personally to know what direction the consultation process could turn. The SIFM acronym is a quality tool to be used to uncover, to engage, to build rapport, and to fact find when beginning the consultation process as a fitness professional.

Support

You need to obtain information on who is in the prospect's life supporting them during their fitness journey. Whether it's husband, wife, kids, coworkers, friends, or someone else, find out. Question how long they have been supportive in their lives. This question will unveil information about their personal life and how things operate outside of the gym. This is a great time to inquire about their nutritional practices as well. Here are some example questions that should be addressed when it comes to support and diet.

1. Does anyone at home work out?
2. Is your spouse supportive of you working out?
3. Who cooks in the household?
4. How many times do they cook throughout the week?
5. Do you eat breakfast?
6. What's the latest you eat in a day?

The answers to these questions will give you a good idea of what is going on in the home environment and how the environment can play a role in the prospect's results or future decision-making.

Internal Reasoning / X-Factor

Why, why, why? What is the underlying emotional reason for the prospect getting to their goals. This is the next piece of information to gather as a fitness professional in the consultation appointment … the *why*.

What is motivating the prospect to work out and start to achieve their goals? Finding the x-factor will be a challenging quest for most fitness professionals. The x-factor is a variable in a given situation that could have the most significant impact on the outcome. This must be an emotional answer, not a superficial answer such as "to be healthy" or "to get toned." Dig, dig, and dig to find what their internal reason is. It may take three or four whys to initiate the prospect to reveal their emotional reasoning. Here are a few internal reasons for wanting to work out or start a program.

1. "I will feel *happier* if I am healthier."
2. "I will stop *feeling unattractive* when I put on certain clothes."
3. "I want to feel more *confident/secure* with my body."

These are some of the keywords and answers that represent a valid internal reason for a prospect wanting to work out or start a program. As a trainer, obtaining their internal reason is very important due to the sensitivity it brings to the prospect. This is their motive for their behavior change, which you will use as a tool to resurge their motivation and influence their thinking when it comes time to select to train with you. This brings more leverage your way when influencing the prospect to begin to work with you. This internal reason will be reiterated in the initial consultation during a later phase, so paying attention to the internal reason and committing it to memory is highly recommended.

What if you can't retrieve the internal reason from a prospect? There are some people who aren't willing to open up or discuss certain things about their life because you are a stranger or they're just a closed person. Keeping this in mind, making a friend will make a sale. Finding commonality and assuring results will be the best method of attempting to open them up until the demonstration workout. Once the endorphins begin to secrete through the body from the demo workout or fitness analyses, more than likely the prospect will become more talkative. Don't be alarmed if they refuse to unveil their internal reason initially, because it will be discovered later. Keep a persistent attitude of wanting to help, keep questioning their why, and the x-factor will be unveiled.

Fun

What hobbies do they have? Whether it is skateboarding, golf, running, bowling, or dancing, knowing their hobbies will assist with identifying how they spend time. The activity or hobby may be done better or at a higher performance with your assistance. This is important information because it can be related to their internal reason if high emotions are related to how they speak of their hobby. This is a great opportunity to build rapport and commonality with the prospect. If they like golfing, then find something in your personal life that relates to golf and converse about it. This commonality brings a sense of rapport to the environment and to the relationship-building process.

Money/Occupation

A seasoned fitness professional will begin to discuss personal monetary value in the early stages of the consultation. The efficient fitness professional will have a good idea of what type of buyer is in front of them to know how to direct the remainder of the sales process. The fitness professional should immediately begin the thought process of what type of program would fit best for their monetary situation without causing a burden. Too many fitness professionals do not touch upon this area and are surprised and alarmed when the prospect objects to starting a program due to financial restraints. The fitness professional must psychologically understand what type of buyer is in front of them.

Consumer behavior research shows that there are three types of buyers based upon pain thresholds.[26]

1. Unconflicted (61%) = average spenders
2. Tightwads (24%) = people who spend less that average before they hit their maximum "buying pain"
3. Spendthrifts (15%) = people who are able to buy more before they hit their "buying pain"

Research also concluded that tightwads are one-fourth of consumers, so learning some strategies for selling to tightwads will be necessary to assure success as a fitness professional.[26] We will dive into the specifics of selling to tightwads in chapters 4 and 5 about price presentations and overcoming objections.

What does the prospect do for a living? Are they sitting behind a desk or on their feet all day? This information will also assist the fitness professional with program design to aid with overused muscles from daily activity. Certain corrective exercises may be needed to help strengthen posture and modify movement imbalances from overused muscles. How they spend their money also relates to spending habits and behavioral practices. There are certain questions that must be answered to obtain spending habits, as with the nutritional inquiries above. For example, how many times do they go out per week? How often do they cook?

All in all, in order to gain value with the prospect, every prospect in their initial consultation must go through an SIFM process. This process should take somewhere between fifteen and thirty minutes. Digging for their internal reason is a must. The information obtained may be needed in the closing stage when the prospect brings up objections. Holding the prospect accountable for every answer given is also crucial. Writing down every answer allows you to remember, and it also shows a sense of professionalism. Honesty and genuineness are needed in this stage because of the relationship rapport that is built. Practice searching for commonality and generating small talk. Active listening will also be a valuable skill needed; let the prospect talk, and remember that research says that talking about oneself is rewarding. The more they talk, the more they feel they can trust and be comfortable around you.

More Example Questions to Begin Building Rapport; Fact Finding at the Investigative Stage

1. How can I help you achieve your fitness goals?
2. Could you please give me some background to your desired fitness outcomes?
3. Why are you seeking to do this work/project/engagement?
4. Why isn't this particular style/format working for you right now?
5. Can you tell me more about the present situation/problem?
6. How long has it been an issue/problem?
7. How long have you been thinking about this?
8. How is it impacting your organization/customers/staff?

9. How much is the issue/problem costing you in time/money/resources/staff/energy?
10. How much longer can you afford to have the problem go unresolved?
11. When you went to your existing supplier and shared your frustrations about this problem, what reassurances did they give you that it wouldn't be repeated?
12. How did these problems/issues first come about? What were the original causes?
13. How severe is the problem?
14. Why do you think the issue/problem has been going on for so long?
15. When do you need the issue/problem fixed by?

CHAPTER 3

INITIAL CONSULTATION / FITNESS ANALYSES / DEMO WORKOUT

Objectives

Understanding and mastering

- measurement tools to use during assessment
- declaring goals
- benefits of building self-efficacy

- principles of the demo workout

Transition from Getting to Know the Client to the Demo Workout

Once the fitness professional goes through the SIFM process and has collected enough behavioral practices and personal information, they must transition to the fitness analyses and demo workout. Every fitness analysis and demo workout will be based on the fitness professional's scope of practice, niche, and client goals. The fitness analyses are important to assess if the prospect is functionally and structurally capable of getting to desired goals. The client may want to increase their bench press, but if after a postural assessment, you notice that they have an extreme upper cross syndrome, the program design may change a bit to address that postural issue. What gets measured gets improved!

As a fitness professional over the last twelve years, I've witnessed a great deal of value lost with clients because the fitness professional doesn't set or collect baseline or initial subjective information. People want to see differences and changes, whether it is in performance or something more tangible like weight or circumference. For example, yoga, Pilates, boxing, MMA, and swim professionals may have various assessment tools in regard to measuring for performance rather than someone just trying to get lean. Remember, the goal is to gain leverage as the authoritative expert in the sales process by collecting as much information/data tying into their x-factor as possible.

Measurement Tools in Fitness

- weight
- BF%
- postural assessments: plumb line
- movement assessments: overhead squat assessment, FMS, single leg squat assessment
- computation of lean body mass
- circumference measurements: waist, hips, shoulders, and so on
- cardio test ex: one-mile run, three-minute step test
- muscular endurance test ex: push-ups, pull-ups, grip

- flexibility test
- performance tests: agility (upper and lower body), coordination, balance

These tests are tools to be used as a gauge to analyze their fitness progress. These basic tools that are used to gauge fitness levels will be used as standards to assist clients with their internal reason. Whether you are a yoga instructor or Pilates instructor, finding a measurement gauge will be crucial when setting goals and sharing concerns.

Nontraditional Measurement Tools (Pilates, Yoga, Boxing, Swimming)

Pilates: a teaser might be an assessment instead of a push-up test. It is better designed for Pilates evaluation.

Yoga: A Warrior 1 or Vinyasa Sun Salutation flow might be a measurement to gauge their level of fitness based on yoga practice.

Boxing: Punch techniques and footwork drills can be tailored into an assessment type of workout for boxing.

Swimming: Video stroke analysis is a great tool for people wanting to learn how to swim.

The measurement tests mentioned are some examples of nontraditional ways of measuring and identifying the prospect's fitness level based on their goal.

All tests must be documented and saved for record keeping. Inform the prospect that taking the tests monthly or bimonthly is necessary for future accountability.

Labeling / Declaration of Goals (Short/Long-Term)

Once all tests and stats have been collected, go through each one and set standards; label them and give a timeline that they will be completed or improved. *Labeling* the client at this time will be of great value.[28] Consumer behavior research shows that internal labeling will cause participants to participate more if they are "grouped."[28] For example, after a prospect completes his push-up test, you can group him as an athlete, beginner, moderate, or example. Research shows that grouping will make people more receptive to messages.[28] Another example is to label a client as superior or a gold member or on different levels.

An Example of Labeling:

"Mrs. Jones, you did an amazing job with your push-ups. You completed over forty in one minute! That's amazing!
"Mrs. Jones, we'll consider you as an athlete when it comes to your upper body strength, and we definitely want to maintain that or even get stronger."

People like being a part of groups that imply some superior quality or level of status that they approve of. Even when the reason is artificial or biased, people tend to take action when they are a part of an elite group of people.[28] As a fitness professional, use the leverage of your credibility and your authoritative stance to label your future clients. They will take more action once they know they are a part of an elite or high-status group.

The *declaration of goals* is a great psychological tool used to acknowledge what results are to come. The psychology behind the declaration of goals is having the ability to create immediate stimulation for the brain.[29] Informing the prospect of what could happen with results in the short term is vital for brain stimulation.[29] The fitness professional must allow the client to envision the problem being solved right away.[29] If the prospect knows their dilemma is being solved, they will be more enticed to purchase.[29]

Research from Ted O'Donoghue and Mathew Rabin in the *Journal of Behavioral Decision Making* also concludes that there is a mass of evidence that people are characterized by a preference for immediate gratification and self-control problems.[30] An implicit theme throughout our discussion is a classification of situations where a preference for immediate gratification is likely to have significant implications. These situations have something in common: they all involve incremental day-to-day (or moment-to-moment) decisions of how to behave now. A person decides whether to have another cigarette right now, to do a minor task today, or to buy a quart of ice cream to eat soon.[30] Such small-scale day-to-day decisions are where self-control problems are most likely to influence behavior. This is the perfect time as a fitness professional to set short-term and long-term goals.

Exercise psychology research also shows that setting short-and long-term goals will increase motivation.[32] Short-term goals are important because they focus on small improvements and provide continuous feedback.[32] The continuous feedback from the short-term goals serves a motivational function and allows for adjustment of goals.[32]

Setting specific goals is very crucial to the outcome and the likeliness of the future prospect becoming your long-term client. From a research perspective, athletes who use process and performance goals rather than outcome goals exhibit less anxiety, greater levels of confidence, enhanced concentration, greater satisfaction, and improved performance (Kingston & Hardy, 1997; Pierce & Burton, 1998) *Journal of Applied Sports Psychology*, 10, S135. As a fitness professional, determining what type of goal to set will boost your value, and performance-type goals will lead to overall less stress in comparison to outcome goals.[31]

As a fitness professional, this was my go-to line; as I was taking their measurements, I would chatter: *"Mrs. Jones, if you continue to watch your saturated fat and extra sugar at night and we continue these workouts, within two weeks you will lose two inches off your waist."* This must be voiced with confidence and assurance. Prospect engagement in setting their goals will be a key indicator on whether they see value in your declaration. Gaining a commitment at this is necessary before you complete a demo workout.

Examples of commitment phrasing follow.

- *"If we start a routine and you cut down on the amount of fats and sugars you consume, you can lose three inches off your waist in less than three weeks. Can we commit to getting this done?"* (This is a short-term, outcome goal.)
- *"Imagine getting your BF percent down 4 to 6 percent in two months."* (This is an outcome goal.)
- *"How would you feel in one month if you were a new dress size?"* (This is a short-term, outcome goal.)
- *"Mrs. Jones, after practicing this active stretching routine, you will be able to touch your toes with ease."* (This is a performance goal.)
- *"Mrs. Jones, your run time will decrease once we have more mobility and stability within your lumbo pelvic hip complex."* (This is a performance goal.)

Most of the answers you should receive are, "Yes, I can't wait," "Sure thing," and "Let's do it." That's when they have verbalized their initial commitment to their goals. And you have taken ownership of their goals. A short-term goal should be set as well as a long-term goal. It is a parallel commitment with each other. Having a timeline of when goals will be reached is crucial for creating an environment of urgency.

Self-Confidence / Self-Efficacy / Imagery

As a successful fitness professional, having the skill set of building and instilling confidence into a person will be needed throughout your career. Increasing self-efficacy or a situational form of self-confidence will be a skill that will be developed over time. Gill (2002) suggests that the most consistent difference between elite and less successful performance is that elite athletes possess greater levels of self-efficacy.[34] This is a vital time in the consultation because it shows how self-confident the prospect is in reaching their goal and how they perceive themselves. As a fitness professional, if you can get the prospect to believe that they can reach the goals, they will be more likely to have successful performance. This is a powerful tool for the fitness professional, as most people can't believe in themselves and see their goals being accomplished, but you can. Be the visionary; be the one who can see it for them.

Using imagery to assist with self-efficacy can be helpful as well. There are two types of imagery techniques to use: MG-M and MS.[37] MG-M (Motivational General Mastery) imagery represents coping and mastering certain situations, for example, being mentally tough during competition. MS is motivational-specific imagery that represents specific goals and behaviors. Most fitness professionals should adopt the MS type of imagery to help future prospects envision the outcome of their behaviors.[37]

According to Bandura (1977), vicarious experiences are the second most powerful technique to improve self-efficacy (see figure 1). The tools utilize by sports psychologists to promote these vicarious experiences are imagery and observation.[35] Other research by Callow, Hardy, and Hall (1998) found that MG-M imagery significantly improved sports confidence in two out of three elite badminton players, and it stabilized the other players' confidence. Help them see it; help the client gain some faith and self-efficacy by asking them to imagine what it is going to feel like accomplishing their goals.

Remember that as a trainer, you are a motivator and an adviser. The most successful trainers are the ones who can embellish reality and give the prospect a view that they can't see themselves. This reminds me of a very successful trainer by the name of Chris Noble. He was awesome at motivating and getting his clients to see positives, whether within their performance or body composition. He was the biggest cheerleader I have ever seen in my fifteen-year career in fitness. The emotional and inspirational power he had were unmatched. After working out with him for just one hour, you would think that you could take over the world. His program design wasn't the most pristine, but the way he made you feel about the workout and yourself was priceless. Every day I would witness Chris just making people feel better; whether it was a smile, a high five, or talking a little junk, he knew what to do to get the best out of people. Imagery was a great tool that Chris would constantly use with his clients. Chris became a top ten trainer in the city and eventually moved on to a modeling career.

Examples of imagery follow.

- *"Imagine getting your BF percent down 4 to 6 percent in two months."* (This is an outcome goal.)
- *"How would you feel in one month if you were a new dress size?"* (This is a short-term, outcome goal.)

All in all, once subjective information has been collected in the consultation, begin to use psychological tools of *imagery* and setting specific short-and long-term goals. Instilling confidence and the belief that they can reach all their goals will be a skill developed over time by the successful fitness professional. Once we get them to just *believe* and *imagine* the goals being met, they must taste what the process is going to feel like in order to reach their goals. The demonstration workout will be the platform for that process.

Demo Workout

The demo workout is the test drive for your services. The prospect has declared their goals, and now you must demonstrate how these goals will be reached with a workout that will illustrate your strengths and value as a trainer. The demo workout is also a tool used to evaluate imbalances and weakness within the body. Six to ten exercises should be enough to evaluate the entire body—the core, the lower body, and the upper body. After the demo workout is complete, you will refer to the weaknesses and strengths you saw during the workout. Remember, you are not just somebody trying to get a sale; you are an expert in your field. A great demo workout has an aspect of *strategic assessing* as well. The demo workout must be precise, exact, and intense to a certain extent. The workout must create a situation of *dependence* on your knowledge and program design. During this time, tie-down questions can be used as a tool to gain more commitment from the prospect. Here are a few keys to the demo workout.

- trainer dependence
- compound movements
- manual resistance exercises (unless using machine for corrective purposes special pop)

FORM AND TECHNIQUE

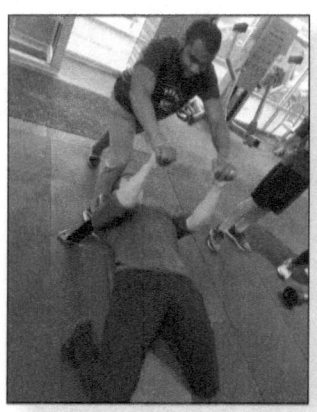

- supersets
- proximity rule
- physical contact / palpation skills
- energy / positive affirmations
- tie-downs
- high intensity

Trainer Dependence

Dr. Ryan Howes, a clinical psychologist at Fuller Graduate School of Psychology, claims that there are two main reasons why clients can become dependent in psychotherapy. The first is an illness or trauma, and the second is the wellness model.[39] As fitness professionals, we are

FORM AND TECHNIQUE

in the class of the wellness model for gaining the dependence of a client. Dependency is about quality, not quantity. The wellness model includes higher physical potential and making a good life even better. One client could have a totally enmeshed dependency after three sessions, while another could spend twenty years in therapy and maintain a healthy sense of individuality.[39] The same rule applies to the fitness profession. Generating dependence can build a long-lasting relationship that can lead to client retention and ultimately a highly valued relationship.

In my experience managing and being a trainer I've seen trainer dependency at its height. Clients can be so loyal and dependent that no matter where the trainer went, the client would follow. If the trainer decided to move twenty miles north of the city, the client would find a way to meet with them with the same frequency as when they were on the south side of the city. The perseverance of the client and commitment to a better overall well-being is the true nature of trainer dependency.

How is the relationship functioning? Can the client make fitness decisions on their own? If the fitness professional isn't present, will the client be self-sufficient? These are all crucial analysis questions when thinking about trainer dependence. Dr. Howes explains that there is *healthy dependency*, and I am in total agreement with him. Healthy dependency requires the fitness professional to provide stable, empowering, supporting, and correct guidance. A client will look for your inspiration in times of need. All in all, as a fitness professional, you are looking for the overall well-being of the client to be the main focus, not just renewal of a package.

Trainer dependency begins with the demo workout—was it fun? Was the workout conducive to the prospect's goals that they mentioned earlier? Did the client feel an aspect of *success* in the workout, or did they feel like they failed? Does the client feel like they can *progress*? These are all crucial mental formations that are forming during the workout to create a dependent client. All in all, as the fitness professional, you are the therapist, and you generate dependency for your client for these reasons: to assist the client with self-love, to become a model for their children/spouse, to build confidence, to enable that in every session the client can focus on themselves and hit that fitness goal, and to assist with expressing emotion. There are plenty more reasons out there, and a high-quality fitness professional can generate a healthy level of dependence. It all begins with the demo workout.

Compound Movements

Compound exercises are multijoint movements that work several muscles or muscle groups at one time. A great example of a compound exercise is the squat exercise, which engages many muscles in the lower body and core, including the quadriceps, the hamstrings, the calves, the glutes, the lower back, and the core. Compound exercises recruit the most muscles, and the more muscles that are recruited, the more calories are burned. Seventy percent of prospects want to increase caloric expenditure.

Manual Resistance Exercises

Manual resistance exercises are exercises that involve the trainer as the source of resistance rather than a bar or machine. Manual resistance exercise will add to the idea of *trainer dependence* in a literal format. No equipment is needed, meaning space is not an issue, nor is time.[38] Manual resistance exercises also create a dependency on the trainer being there for the prospect, which is key in the sales process. You want the prospect to feel like they need you. Another advantage to manual resistance exercises is that the trainer can control the rate of speed and amount of resistance during each phase of the exercise. The technique can be controlled, and the trainer will be the spotter to control the client's range of motion.[38] With manual resistance, training muscles can be worked to temporary exhaustion.[38] If fifty pounds of resistance is needed for the first set, then the trainer can dictate whether the prospect needs more or less for the second and third sets. Muscles can be worked maximally in each rep within a short period of time. My experience in teaching trainers about manual resistance exercises is that they can be done anywhere, and they're inexpensive and time-efficient. You can target any muscle group through manual resistance exercises. A key thing to remember during manual resistance exercises is to communicate with the prospect the proper coordination of the exercises and the perception of resistance.

The value of manual resistance exercise can be very impactful when completing a demo workout. The psychological advantage of showing a client what they can and can't do without the use of equipment will be paramount when conducting a demo workout.

I've seen so many rookie trainers take prospects on the floor and straight to a machine for their workout, which generates no *value* at all. Once you show them a machine for their workout, they will realize that no more help is needed since they have the machine. As a fitness professional, you are the *resistance*. Here are a few examples.

Supersets

A superset is when one *set* of an exercise is performed directly after a *set* of a different exercise without rest between them. Once each superset is complete, then rest for one and a half to two minutes to recover. It is important to measure the pace when completing supersets. If the prospect is beginning to get exhausted, slow the pace down. On the other hand, if the prospect doesn't seem to be challenged, then increase the intensity of the exercise. Keep in mind the demo workout is intended for the prospect to be tested.

Proximity Rule

Personal training is *personal*, so as a trainer, you are being invited into someone's personal space. Take advantage and make sure that you are in close physical contact with the prospect at all times during the demo workout. The principle of proximity is the tendency for people to form social relationships with individuals who are physically closer to them.[40] Proximity means how close an object or person is physically to you.

People in face-to-face meetings command one another's attention and feel involved with group tasks. The attention we pay to those present tends to make our interactions with them more memorable than our interactions with those far away (Latane, Liu, Nowak, & Bonevento, 1995).[41] The presence of others increases conformity through its effect on felt surveillance and social pressure. In the famous Milgram experiments (e.g., 1974), when an experimenter and subject were in the same room, about 65 percent of the subjects obeyed the experimenter's command to give 450-volt electric shocks to a "poor learner" (a confederate). However, when the experimenter left the room and gave his commands by telephone, only 20 percent were obedient to the 450-volt level.[40] Milgram also tried changing the proximity of the subjects to the victim. When the subjects were seated right next to the victim, only 40 percent of the subjects were obedient and shocked the victim to the 450-volt level. Thus, if the experimenter was close to the subjects, his authority was strong, but if the victim was close to the subjects, then the victim's protests overrode the demands of the experimenter.

The research backs up the claims of how proximity can be beneficial and influential to relationship and group interaction.[40] Whether it is face-to-face or frequency of spontaneous interaction, proximity can have tremendous benefit, especially as a fitness professional.

There should be undivided attention toward the prospect. A two-foot distance should be between you and the prospect at all times. Proximity = *value*! As a trainer, you are literally there by their side. When conducting the demo workout, spotting every flexion and extension in an exercise and shift of the body will be an important aspect in the training dependency.

Physical Contact / Palpation Skills

Physical contact will be necessary as a trainer for spotting and correcting form. Having the skill of palpation of certain muscle groups to make sure that they are firing is crucial in building value and credibility in your assessment of movement in the demo workout. *This is a skill that will need to be learned and practiced* like any other tool in this book. Physical therapists, athletic trainers, and orthopedic doctors all use the skill of palpation for general assessments, and as a fitness professional, you can too.

In 2010 the American Massage Therapy Association published a very informative article by Joseph E. Muscolino on muscle palpation. It stated

> The term *palpation* comes from the Latin term *palpare*, which literally means to touch.[42] However, in the context of muscular assessment, palpation involves much more than simply touching the muscle. Muscular palpation

has two major objectives. The first is to locate the target muscle that is being palpated.[42] Once it has been located, the second objective is to assess its health by feeling for its tone and texture: Is it tight or loose? Are there trigger points located within it? Is it inflamed or tender to touch? Are fascial adhesions present? …

Guideline No. 1: Know the Attachments of the Target Muscle

The first guideline is to know the attachments of the target muscle that is being palpated. Knowing the attachments is the first necessary step because it gives us the general location of where to place out palpating fingers.

Simply put, we palpate between the muscle's attachments. For example, if the target muscle is the deltoid, knowing that it attaches from the lateral clavicle, acromion process, and spine of the scapula to the deltoid tuberosity of the humerus, tells us to place our palpating fingers between the scapular/clavicular attachment and the deltoid tuberosity (Figure 1, left).

More specifically, if we want to palpate the anterior deltoid, we place our palpating fingers just distal to the lateral clavicle. If we want to palpate the middle deltoid, we place our fingers just distal to the acromion process.…

Guideline No. 2: Know the Actions for the Target Muscle

When the target muscle contracts, it hardens and becomes palpably clearer. Continuing with the deltoid as our example, if we know the muscle's actions, we know what to ask the client to do to make it contract: We ask the client to abduct their arm at the glenohumeral joint. The deltoid contracts and becomes palpably harder, allowing us to palpate its entirety and more easily discern it from the adjacent musculature.

When completing a repetition or set, palpating can assure that the correct muscle is being contracted or engaged. If the prospect is performing an exercise and begins to sway off-balance, you are there to support them and get them right back on track. If you're conducting a step up, have them place their hand on your shoulder. Provide physical support anytime there is a need. Even overexaggerate the spotting as well, because it will only bring more value to the demo workout and you as a trainer. As a fitness professional, think about as many spotting techniques as you can come up with. Palpation literacy and spotting will be paramount when conducting a demo workout to provide value and credibility as a *true* fitness professional.

Dr. Feeney

A true master of his craft, Tom Feeney was one of the best trainers I have seen. Tom was amazing at educating his clients and making them aware of what muscles were being engaged and which ones weren't. He taught his clients what proper movement was supposed to feel like. Looking from the outside in, his sessions looked a bit mundane and boring because it wasn't the normal high-intensity circuit training that most trainers indulge in, but if any of his peers got an opportunity to dive into his session, they would see how scripted and detailed his programming was. Every movement was paid close attention to. His attention to detail surpassed any trainer I've hired or worked with by far. Whether it was a conventional bird dog / quadruped or a simple protraction of the scapula, Tom was able to allow the client to feel and become aware of the correct muscle movement and how it was engaged. His hands were constantly engaging in muscle movement and contractions. He wanted his client to *feel* every movement and understand the goal of the movement. Nothing would throw off his attention; he gave full observation and heed to his client, which generated his value as an elite trainer. He was a pure genius, with incredible patience and an overall eye for training. He had over fifteen years of experience, so being able to palpate and engage certain muscles was well-practiced. When I was his fitness director, he averaged over 115 sessions per month, which equated to $85,000 in recognized revenue, paying attention to every movement and muscle being engaged. He was a constant professional. I would call Tom Dr. Feeney due to his patience and his ability to program a design for a client no matter the goals. In addition he was amazing at his online marketing and overall professionalism. Of course, my journey with Tom didn't last very long as he was promoted to become a fitness director and run his own team. Tom was very smart and influential when it came to being a leader among his trainer peers!

Energy / Positive Affirmations

Being a motivator is what you're selling in the long run. Having high energy is an added value that will keep the prospect motivated to want to work with you. Having an upright posture, hands out in front, clapping, high fiving, and positive affirmations are all examples of having good energy. Energy is transferable and can truly be felt by the prospect.

Researchers have looked for and found neural evidence to back up the hypotheses for why positive affirmation works as well as it does. Positive self-affirmation is the recognition and assertion of the existence and value of one's individual self. It is believed to be beneficial because it's rewarding and pleasurable, and it works because it acts as a defense mechanism by reminding us of the things in life that we cherish, thereby broadening the foundation of our self-worth.[47] Specifically, participants in the self-affirmation condition exhibited greater activation in parts of the brain that are known to be involved in expecting and receiving reward (the ventral striatum and the ventral medial prefrontal cortex) than did those in the control group. Also, when thinking about what they most valued in a future context (e.g., "Think about a time in the future when you will have fun with family and friends"), but not in a past context, the positive-affirmation group showed more activity in areas associated with thinking about the self (the medial prefrontal cortex and posterior cingulate cortex).

Positive affirmation statements include the following.

- *"You can do it."*
- *"That is pretty easy for you."*

- *"Wow, that was pretty good form!"*
- *"Great job on the balance."*

Tie-Downs

Tie-down questions are effective and extremely *powerful* at layering questions to see if the prospect is ready to be closed. This is a very useful and effective tool that should be used during the demo workout to feel the temperature of the prospect to gauge how close they are toward committing to your services. A verbal stimulus influences participants to such an extent that it affects their cognition.[43,44,45] There are thousands of research studies out there in behavioral and motivational research that study how cognition is influenced and how it occurs. The entire process of selling is dependent upon prospects being attentive and contemplating and committing to certain foundational value propositions. In fact, regardless of the product or service, for a prospect to make a positive buying decision, that prospect must first pay attention to what a salesperson is sharing. If this does not occur, the sale will die.

The answers to tie-down questions give the trainer feedback as to where their prospect is in the sales process. As a trainer, selling may be new to you, so having an idea of how close you are to a closed deal is helpful. How do you know if your prospect is understanding what you are sharing? Do they agree with what you are saying? Even when a prospect is on the workout floor, just because they are participating and giving effort in the workout doesn't mean that they are committed or that you know what they are thinking. I've witnessed it millions of times: a prospect will give you the head nod and complete the demo workout with a smile, but when it comes time to begin a program or sign up, they look at you and say, "No." During the entire demo workout, the client might have been actively listening to you or was thinking of something else or just mind wandering. And you feel shocked and alarmed because that wasn't the nonverbal signs you were reading during the workout. You feel like they deceived or fooled you. This lack of awareness or recognition is a downfall for most fitness professionals.

To enhance cognition and foster commitment to a persuasive message, one simple, yet highly effective, way is through using what is known as a tie-down.[46] A tie-down is defined as a value-building statement that is converted to a question. Tie-downs are classified as an involvement trial close. Tie-downs are extremely influential because they halt the flow of information and allow prospects to mentally digest and verbally assess an assertion of value.[46] This assists the human brain in focusing upon and mentally processing what was presented.

A Tie-Down Study

A study conducted by Kevin Blankership and Traci Craig at Purdue University examined how contextual factors, such as characteristics of the communicator, moderate whether tag questions (tie-downs) act "powerless." The study manipulated source credibility, tag question use, and argument quality. When the source was low in credibility, tag questions (tie-downs) use decreased persuasion and biased message processing relative to a control message. However, when the source was credible, tag questions increased message processing in a relatively objective manner. Therefore, it appears that tag questions can have different effects on information processing depending on who uses the tag questions.[45] When the tie-down was communicated by someone viewed as credible and was attached to a compelling message, the research confirmed that the tie-down amplified the persuasive impact of the message. However, the tie-down became counterproductive if it was linked to a weak appeal or if the person conveying the tie-down was not regarded as trustworthy.[46] So before you begin tying people down, trust must be generated.

While giving the demo workout to the client, this is the perfect opportunity to ask various tie-down questions. For example:

- *"Did you feel it in your quads when you bent your legs ninety degrees on the squat?"*
- *"Can you see how this lifting angle can cause more muscle stimulation?"*
- *"Can you see yourself practicing these stretches on your own?"*
- *"Can you see how this workout will drop your BF percent?"*
- *"Can you see yourself working out like this two times per week?"*
- *"Can you feel your chest burn when you hold that push-up?"*

Tie-down questions are a true measurement marker to really see how close you are to closing that prospect. Practicing tie-down questions is a valuable skill needed in the sales process. When used correctly, tie-downs have been scientifically proven to enhance the persuasiveness of a message. Tie-downs also assist fitness professionals in guiding prospects in being attentive to and contemplating the key value propositions that the sale is built upon. Warming the prospect up with qualified questions will allow for a smooth transition into the price presentation.

All in all, the demo workout is important to create dependency with the trainer. The client must feel like they truly need your assistance to help achieve their goals. The workout must be used as a tool to evaluate the prospect on fitness-related issues that you see as a trainer. Every exercise that is completed must have a standard. For example, "You only held the wall sit for thirty seconds; most can do it for a minute." This keeps the prospect at bay with future goals to hit. Maintain a positive stance during the entire demo workout; even when the prospect is fatigued or unable to complete certain exercises, maintain a positive stance. Learning and practicing of tie-down questions will determine how far you are from closing that prospect. As a trainer, you must push the client to fatigue, yet keep them motivated to keep going to the last repetition.

High Intensity

The demo workout is also an opportunity to use high-intensity workouts to gauge and diagnose weaknesses and imbalances within the prospect's body. Weaknesses, such as core strength, lower body endurance, and upper body endurance, are all concerns the trainer should be aware of. A high-intensity workout that causes the HR to rise in a short period of time, muscles anaerobically fatiguing, is a key indicator that cardiovascular and muscular endurance is needed. High-intensity workouts are key because most people will not push themselves that much, which is another point of leverage within the sales process. Keep in mind that depending on the overall fitness level of a prospect, intensity will be varied.

Looking for Concerns

During the time of the demo workout, the client has a chance to move and complete various suggested movements. This is a time to put the doctor's hat on and document everything you see or notice that may be a weakness, imbalance, imperfection, or shortcoming, and even strengths within the demonstration workout. This is what distinguishes fitness professionals from everyone else. For example, the buddy who the client works out with doesn't have the eye for noticing postural alignment issues and muscular imbalances. As fitness professionals, we have the eye for movement inefficiencies. Whether it is knees caving in, low back arching, or erratic breathing, document everything because you will need this valuable information later on in the price presentation. Remember to also document strengths because that can be a positive value added to the end of the session as well, and it has an aura of true *professionalism*.

According to most health professionals, here are the reasons for documenting during a demonstration workout.

- Ensure continuity of care as it serves as a communication tool among health-care providers.
- Plan and evaluate a prospect's treatment.
- Create a permanent record for the patient's future care.
- Create a database to evaluate effectiveness of treatment.

All in all, the demo workout is an opportunity to show your value as a trainer. Your enthusiasm and energy will be transferred to the client as they battle through the demo workout. The demo workout is also a chance to push your client and challenge them in a way that they are not used to when working out. The workout will also give you a temperature of whether they are ready for a trainer by their responses to tie-down questions and the intensity of exercises.

Example Workout

Step-ups 12x each leg
Wall sits 30 seconds (manual resistance: holding hands with the client's palms pressed against each other)

Step-ups variation (abduct leg after step-up)

Wall sit variations (add manual resistance by extending both arms out and holding their fist, simulating a bench press while they are in a wall sit position)

Side shuffles 10–15yds

Squats 25xs

Side shuffles resistance

Squat jumps

Manual shoulder press 25x

Manual push-up 10–15

2rds

Manual dips

Manual curls

2rnds

Lying 6 inches leg holds

Flutter kicks

Russian twist

Planks

Three rounds as many progressions as needed … *Feel the burn … Feel the energy.* Can you feel it? Can you see yourself doing a workout like this two or three times a week?

(Keep in mind this is a basic example circuit workout for someone trying to lose weight or gain some cardiovascular conditioning. You can tailor the workout to be more specific to their goals.)

FORM AND TECHNIQUE

In conclusion, once you have built enough rapport and gained mutual trust through finding similarity and searching for common interest with the prospect, you can begin to take efficient measurements and set goals. Make sure to declare goals that resonate with the client and that are attainable and reachable. If they are losing weight, set more body composition goals; if they are an athlete, set performance goals. Write them down so each of you can see them clearly.

Once goals are declared, it is time for the test drive, the demo workout. Remember the demo workout is the vehicle that will be used to get them to achieve their goals. Challenge but don't overkill, bring energy and enthusiasm, create client dependency with manual resistance exercises, be in close proximity, tie them down to their goals with the actual workout that they are completing, and lastly, use positive affirmations. All of these tools must be practiced like a professional athlete who constantly fine-tunes their game. Peyton Manning, LeBron James, Tom Brady, and Floyd Mayweather are all perfect examples of how to master your craft day in and day out. Be precise and be purposeful when this process is happening. Be mindful of every action and every step you take. This will be the difference between not only receiving a new client but changing someone's life.

CHAPTER 4

PRICE PRESENTATION

Objectives

Understanding and mastering

- transition from workout to prices
- the temperature of your prospect
- rookie trainer mistakes
- steps in a price presentation
- showing prices effectively

Transition from Workout to Prices—Was It Smooth?

Once the demo workout is complete, this is the perfect opportunity to present prices of your program. Most trainers suffer from not showing prices at the proper time or not setting the prospect up correctly to present prices. In other words, there must be a setup process done (tie-downs, rapport building, declaration of goals, generating trainer dependency, and so on) or proper steps taken before you show your prices. At this time in the appointment, you should have a line of rapport, know the prospect's goals, created dependency with the workout, and have an idea (documented) of what concerns (imbalance, postural issues, weaknesses) may be occurring with the client. If you *don't* have the following gathered, I would recommend setting the client up for another appointment to reestablish those key criteria again on another day.

A research group that explored the process and technologies of successful companies determined that the "best in class" companies revolved around skill development in regard to value-based selling.[55] Supporting the sales professional with a formal sales process that will help guide them through the various stages of prospect communication will flow naturally and result in more success.[55] Another skill development listed by "best in class companies" was relationship management skills.[55] Treating the potential prospect like a client before they commit to a signed contract sends a strong positive message about the sales rep potential to provide superior service once the deal is done.[55]

This chapter details a scheme and plan of attack that if practiced will lead to higher closing percentage and greater value being added to your assessment appointment as a fitness professional.

Do You Know the Temperature?

Being unaware of the prospect's temperature or feeling how close they are to commitment is a common mistake in the fitness industry, and it will result in missed opportunities for commitment to your program or simply closing the deal. Awareness, awareness, awareness … are they ready for the price presentation? Really think about and be mindful to this question. *Did they answer the tie-down questions with enthusiasm and positivity? Did they rely on you during the workout? Was the workout rushed? Did they respect and value your declaration of goals? Do you have some type of commonality/rapport with them?* During the first couple of steps of the appointment, there should be an invisible flow of smoothness that is unruffled throughout the first couple of steps. If the answer is "No," then you must reset and accomplish the latter at a later date to increase your chances of commitment to your program. Remember, this is like the quarterback looking back at the game film understanding the coverages and seeing what he has to do to get better. This is the dancer looking at every foot placement in her choreography to ensure elegance and gracefulness. Fitness professionals are true professionals, and looking at our blind spots will allow for more efficiency and increasing success. Never blame the prospect; take accountability for mastering your craft.

Know Your Worth / Know Your Numbers

Before we begin going over the setup of the price presentation, let's talk about prices. As a trainer, you must know how much you're worth. Whether it is ninety dollars a hour or forty-five dollars for thirty-minute six-packs, twelve-packs, or thirty-two-packs, know all of your options like the back of your hand. This is important because there may be times when you have to create a budgeted program for a client. I have all my new trainers memorize how much it would cost for them to train 1x 2x 3x and even 4x's. Having all these numbers in the back of your head will be easier when it's time to create a program that fits someone's budget. You must have various options ready to present at any time. Prepare for the battle! Know all your numbers by heart! Some clients may be able to afford the largest package, and some may not. Selling a prospect one session a month for twelve months is as valuable as a twelve-pack of sessions. The idea is to have programs that will be able to fit anyone's budget.

Rookie Trainer Mistake

I have seen this situation too many times, so naming names is just irrelevant with this story. Let's just call the subject Rookie Trainer. Rookie Trainer has successfully built rapport, a successful demo workout has declared all the goals, and RT brings the prospect back to the assessment office. Now keep in mind, time is the enemy because the prospect has to catch the train, and it's a Friday before Thanksgiving break. Rookie Trainer begins to present prices, and the client asks, "Can we do something a little smaller?" Rookie Trainer hesitates, gets nervous, and replies, "I'll be back. Let me see." His boss isn't around, and he is urgently looking for a price card to review with his ready-to-purchase client. After about three minutes of searching and seeking for a price card, he finally finds a price card of other packages, and on his way back, the prospect is walking out. "I have to catch the train. I'll shoot you an email, and we will talk more next week."

Rookie Trainer didn't think about the fact that it's Thanksgiving weekend, and it might be another seven or eight days before he sets up another appointment again with that client. The opportunity was right in his hands; he was minutes away from having success and closing a client. What halted his flow? Not knowing his worth. Not knowing the options he could have given right at that moment. The lesson is to have all options readily available; go to battle fully prepared for *anything*. All fitness professionals should have all numbers down pat and ready to present. At any moment, you might have to rattle off the best options for your client.

Six Steps to Follow in Presenting Prices

There are six steps to follow in presenting prices to the prospect. Each step is important in the closing aspect of the sale process. Try not to miss a step or skip steps. Take your time to ensure that your presentation will lead to a closed deal.

Step 1: Confirmation of Workout (Clarifying Questions)

Once the prospect has completed the workout, your transition into the price presentation *begins*! I have learned the best way to transition the prospect from the workout floor to another location is to simply say, *"That was a great workout. Let's sit for a second to go over a few things from the workout."* Sit them down, usually in the original room you were in to take body weight and measurements. Immediately you want to highlight the highs and lows of the workout. You also want the prospect to acknowledge what they learned, the aspects of accountability, and how having the correct intensity will assist them to reach their goals. Example open-ended questions to begin a brief assessment and recognition of the workout follow.

- *How do you feel?* This relates to *intensity recognition*. (Do you think you can train at that intensity level every time you come into the gym?)
- *Do you feel like you could have created that workout on your own?* This relates to *knowledge recognition*. (Do you feel like you have enough knowledge to put together a workout like that?)
- *Can you see yourself working out like that two or three times a week?* This relates to *accountability recognition*.
- *When was the last time you worked out like that?* This again relates to *intensity recognition*.
- *What was the hardest part of the workout?*
- *What was the easiest part of the workout?*

If the demo workout was completed correctly, answers like "I've never worked out like this before," "This was great," or "I loved it" should come up. Those are all reactions that a prospect should have when finished with the demo workout. They should be sweating and feeling a little buzz from the intensity of the exercises. If they aren't responding close to the nature of the previous statements, then there was something missing within the demo workout, whether it was the intensity or maybe the exercise wasn't challenging enough. Ninety percent of all prospects will respond to high-intensity manual resistance workouts by getting tired and admitting the difficulty of the workout. Determining how they feel will allow you to know how to steer your concerns, which is the next step.

Step 2: Identifying Concerns (Put On the Doctor's Hat)

As a trainer, you are skilled in increasing strength, increasing cardiovascular endurance, losing weight, increasing flexibility, toning, firming, and so on. The fitness professional must also become skilled at recognizing weaknesses (muscular, cardiovascular), imbalance, postural deviations, and arthrokinematic misalignments as well. The skill of "putting on the doctor's hat" will be profound, heartfelt, and keen to the presentation. Putting on the doctor's hat is basically to act as one would in one's particular profession while in a different setting. You have to put yourself in a "bearer of bad news" frame of mind, regardless of whether you are a real doctor or not. This is a true skill that can be profound and generate a lot of value in the appointment.

Rookie Trainer Mistake: Having No Concerns = No Value

In the beginning of my career as a young, fit lad, I was never able to get commitment from peers my own age. They always had excuses, and I never got commitment. Was it me? Was it my workouts? It was none of the above. The problem was I never put on my doctor's hat. I was pretty good at developing rapport but never offered or showed any concern because they were my peers and they were pretty healthy. I finally got tired of not getting commitment from prospects around my age, and I finally figured out I was not putting on my doctor's hat. I began to really observe my play-by-play and noticed the weakness and imbalance that were occurring during the demo workouts of my peers. I made it an objective of mine to really place emphasis on putting on my doctor's hat during my price presentations. When it was time to offer concerns, I would take a deep breath and slow down my speech, really changing the entire atmosphere from fun and high energy to 100 percent seriousness. There was no smiling and no more giggling; the rapport building was over with. I was fully aware that my concerns would be my value. It worked with my peers, and they developed a respect for my profession. Even if they couldn't afford the program, they felt that they needed the training due to my concern for their well-being. It was astonishing how a little concern and imitating a doctor assisted with my business growth.

With that said, if the prospect doesn't want or need any of the previous, you have little or no value. Once the prospect has identified that they haven't worked out like that in a while or that it was different from their normal routine, identify concerns that you had throughout the workout. Mental notes or physically writing notes on weaknesses and imbalances observed within the workout will come into play at this time during the sales presentation. Sharing with the prospect what you as an expert feel needs to be worked on brings value. Whether it was their core strength, lower body endurance, upper body strength, or whatever, have at least three things that you viewed as weaknesses or imbalances and share them with the prospect. Here are some examples of putting on the doctor's hat and presenting concerns.

- *"Mr. Jones, I have a few concerns. While you were performing the plank exercise, I noticed that your back was sinking to the ground, which signifies a weak core and lower back. We must get that improved. Will this work for you?"*
- *"Mrs. Jackson, I noticed while you were working out that you were holding your breath throughout the routine. We are going to have to work on more fluid breathing when your muscles meet stress. This will help to oxygenate the muscles and keep them working. Will this work for you?"*
- *"Mrs. Hill, while you were performing your push-ups, you were barely able to bend the elbow to ninety degrees. We are going to have to build more upper body strength, but if we keep working on it and learning exercises, you'll get there in no time."*

While sharing concerns, always maintain a positive tone and speak about the concerns as issues that you as a trainer have dealt with before and will resolve.

Be 100 percent transparent in the first part of expressing the concern, but also sharing with the prospect a resolution is key. Speak about the concerns with confidence and assurance that you will help them reverse the issue at hand. Asking the client if it will work for them brings a joint affair to the resolution. They either agree or disagree. You are not simply telling them, but you are also exploring and planning the resolution together. Say something positive, share the concern, and then proceed to another positive statement. No concerns equals no value!

FORM AND TECHNIQUE

Step 3: Review of Goals and Taking Ownership

Once you have stated your concerns, review previous goals that were set earlier during fitness analyses. Go over dates of goals and measurements or results expected. Quickly state that a nutrition change will also have to occur. During the analyses' review of measurements or whatever was tested, speaking using assumption techniques will be important. Here are a few examples.

- *"Once we begin your program, two inches will melt off."*
- *"Once we continue your training, you will notice an immediate change in your endurance."*
- *"Once we start this program, your back will feel much better."*
- *"Once we begin this program, your arms will be toned up in six weeks."*

You're not only reviewing the goals and measurements but verbally implanting the idea of reaching these goals with your assistance.

Taking ownership of their goals will make the relationship build. According to the National Bureau of Economic Research, "firms with employee ownership tend on average to match or exceed the performance of other similar firms."[50] Their research shows that a higher human resource index number of employees invested at a firm results in greater worker-reported work effort and better company performance. It also supports the idea that cooperative culture can be fostered by ownership, which drives better workplace performance.[50] Taking ownership is about taking initiative of the client's goals. We take ownership when we believe that taking action is not someone else's responsibility. You, as the fitness professional, are accountable for the quality and timeliness of an outcome, even when you're working with others. You care about the outcome the same way you would care as an owner of the organization.[51] Taking ownership is establishing expectations and defining what success looks like. This means defining the end goal. What end result do you want the prospect to achieve? By focusing on the end goal, you are placing trust in your prospect, and that trust empowers them.[51]

Trust should be established between the prospect and the trainer during discussion of goals. Listening to the prospect will be influential as well to create an environment of mutual respect. Keep in mind that most goals will be set based off concerns drawn from the demo workout, which are also mentioned after the workout. Your tone and confidence will play a big part in this aspect of the assessment.

Am I Really the Owner of Their Goals?

This idea brings me to a story of Chris W. I was a brand-new fitness director taking on clients, and I had a consult with a middle-aged African American male named Chris. He was very interested in losing weight and was highly motivated to reach his goals. He was a comic book artist and had lofty goals for his comic business as well; He was a very creative and genuine type of guy. I built some great rapport with him, even enough to call him a friend. (Remember the *personal* part of personal training.) Of course, he invested in his health by purchasing a three-month training package worth over three thousand dollars. I was fully invested and taking a lot of ownership in his goals. I constantly communicated with him about how he was doing, reminded him of his session start time, set him up with a registered dietitian, and gave him homework assignments.

The first two months of training went as planned, and then the frequency of training started to die down. I would email him and call, and he would promise to show up but never showed up. Keep in mind he still had about a thousand dollars worth of sessions left on his account. I personally felt like I was missing something that was going on in his life, or was it me? Because I was so motivated for him, I began to lose my self-confidence in myself and my ability. Chris finally came in and let it all out. He was struggling with his relationship with his girlfriend and had started to emotionally eat. His job wasn't doing so well, so he abandoned the gym and his goals. It took a few more calls and emails, but after about three months went by, he finally came back in and continued to train. We were basically starting the process all over again.

All in all, as fitness professionals, we can take as much ownership as we want, but know that we are only the fingers pointing people in the right direction. They must be able to look at the direction we are pointing them to and go toward it. Do not get down and do not get discouraged if someone falls off the trail you set. Be available, be positive, and take ownership of just caring and being *there* for that person.

Step 4: Program Recommendations

This is the time for the fitness professional to once again put on a doctor's hat and make a recommendation for the prospect to be successful. As a fitness professional, even if you have never trained anyone before, your recommendation will go a long way. As a true fitness professional, you must give the recommendation with a sense of confidence, assertiveness, and poise. You must act like you have given this recommendation before, which has led clients to being successful with your program. This may take a little practice like everything else in this book, but it will go a long way. A strong recommendation of frequency of training, time commitment, and duration of sessions will be paramount in this aspect of the sales process. Here is the verbatim example of how to suggest a recommendation.

"Now, Mrs. Jones, based on your desired goal of reaching that BF percent goal of 15 percent, based on my professional background, I would recommend you come in the gym and work with me two times a week for sixty minutes each time for the next three months. How does that sound?" (This is a preclosing question.)

This simple and vague recommendation is only the precursor to the next step, which is the mesocycle. As a fitness professional, you must *act as if* you have had clients reach their goals based on this exact recommendation. The act-as-if principle technique is the process of acting like you want to do something, even though you may not feel like doing it.[51] To use this motivation-building trick, you adopt the posture, tone, and physical approach of someone who you imagine would like doing the activity that you are struggling to motivate yourself to do. In this case, as a fitness professional, act as if you have had millions of clients reach their goals based on the recommendation that you have given.

Step 5: Program Design / Mesocycles

The client's program must be centered on a three-month goal minimum or whatever timeline is achievable that you see fit, whether it is to lose body fat, gain strength, or increase their overall cardio endurance. Always present a program in the length of a time, usually a three-month total. Giving a brief but detailed description of how their program will be laid out will also give insight to your knowledge of fitness and exercise programming as a whole. As the trainer, you must be direct and serious when giving your program recommendation. This is when the doctor writes his prescription to his patient, and the patient must adhere to the recommendation of the doctor. Why? Because he knows and trust the doctor's stance on the issue at hand. The same precedent must be set when presenting your program to the client. This is not just a program; this is a prescription that will get you to reach your goals.

Example Mesocycle Plan

"Mrs. Jones, I recommend you seeing me two times a week for sixty minutes each time for the nextthree months in order to reach these goals efficiently.

"This is how your program will be laid out for the next three months.

"There will be three four-week phases.

"The first four-week phase will be mobility and range of motion. We're going to loosen you up and get your muscles stimulated and more functional.

"Your second four-week phase will be muscular endurance. We are going to add resistance training and increase muscle breakdown. This is the phase when the inches change.

"Your third four-week phase will be HIIT training. This is going to take your metabolism to a whole new fat-burning level.

"How does that sound?" This is the key question to ask to ensure that they are in agreement with the plan.

Starting out by discussing how the program will be laid out in three four-week phases will set a precedent to how much commitment will be needed to reach the set goal. Everyone's fitness plan and mesocycle will differ. Someone participating in boxing, yoga, Pilates, or swimming may have different aspects of their mesocycle, but they still need to have a plan in place no matter the modality of fitness. That will be crucial for credibility and experience.

Step 6: Show Prices

This is one of the most important and a crucial step in the art of the sales process. Being able to present your prices smoothly and well polished will determine your success as a fitness professional achieving new clientele. Michael Jordan wanted to take the last shot every time the game was close. He had *no fear*. This is truly a skill of just going out there, diving in, and taking your shot! The price presentation is literally your jump shot; it is your *weapon* for success. I would literally hire a trainer, and before giving them a prospect or new member, they had to have their price presentation memorized and mastered. This technique would make it less painful for my trainers as they began their careers as fitness professionals. Practice, practice, practice will be the key for success.

The price presentation entails explaining your prices and how they work, cancellations, and monthly, bimonthly, or package payments. Make sure you go through your programs thoroughly and smoothly. After explaining your programs, you want to conclude with a closing question, for example, *"Which one of the options makes the most sense to get started with today?"* Try not to stutter, and practice how your tone will sound. Keep in mind that doing a monthly program requires a greater commitment, so a little more explanation will be needed.

Here are a couple of example pricing presentations for various programs. Practice your own by keeping the same principles at play and making sure you always explain cancellations and end with a closing question.

A. **Price Presentation for Various Packages**

"All right, Mrs. Jones, you did a great job on the workout, but there are a few thing we have to work on: your upper body strength and breathing." (Expressing concerns) *"We have to keep challenging your cardiovascular system so we can increase your overall endurance. I have two different options to get this going so we can hit these goals. We can do a one-and-a-half-month program in which we meet two times a week for sixty minutes, which ends*

up being twelve sessions at eight hundred dollars; or a three-month program in which we meet two times a week for sixty minutes, which ends up being twenty-four sessions at nineteen hundred dollars. All programs have a twenty-four hour notice for cancellation. Now, based on your time commitment and budget, which one of these programs makes the most sense for you to get started with it today?"

B. **Price Presentation for Monthly Programs**

"All right, Mrs. Jones, you did a great job on the workout, but there are a few things we have to work on: your balance, core strength, and breathing. We have to keep challenging your cardiovascular system so we can increase your overall endurance. I have three different options to get this going so we can hit these goals. We can do a one-month, three-month, or six-month program. Most people choose the six-month program to guarantee their results. You can meet with me one time a week at one hundred forty dollars per month, two times a week at two hundred eighty dollars per month, or three times a week at four hundred twenty dollars per month. All sessions require a twenty-four-hour notice for cancellation. Now, based on your schedule and budget, which one of these programs makes the most sense for you to get started with it today?

Once you have completed your price presentation, always remain quiet; flip and zip. This technique is used to let the prospect figure out what is the best program for them to commit to based on budget and other variables. It is a very awkward moment of silence, but always remember that the first one to talk loses.

Practicing this basic price presentation verbatim will give you a quality scheme of what a smooth and straight-to-the-point price presentation should detail. Always explain the cancellation policy and prices, and of course what you recommend. The more you set up the prospect by becoming their friend (the liking principle), a declaration of goals, an effective demo workout, and proper questioning, motivation, and tie-downs, the easier the price presentation will be. Here is a quick review of the *full price presentation* once the demo workout is complete.

FORM AND TECHNIQUE

1. *Confirmation questions.* Acknowledge certain aspects of the workout (intensity, accountability, knowledge).
2. *Address concerns.* Identify imbalances, weaknesses, and strengths with the doctor's hat.
3. *Review of goals.* Readdress goals and take ownership.
4. *Offer recommendations.* Act as if you are giving a prescription wearing your doctor's hat.
5. *Program design mesocycle.* Lay out the program in three four-week phases.
6. *Show prices.* Deliver a smooth and polished presentation of the programs that you offer.
7. *Flip and zip.* Flip the prices and program over and let the prospect gauge and evaluate what they feel is best; let them choose. Just wait! *"Now, based on your schedule and budget, which one of these programs makes the most sense for you to get started with it today?"*

Once again, like anything in life, once you practice it enough times, it will become second nature. Becoming a successful fitness professional is truly an art, and like any art form, you must challenge yourself in order to grow. Challenge yourself by mastering this phase and add value to every appointment you have.

Now the price presentation is complete. Next is overcoming objections.

CHAPTER 5

OVERCOMING OBJECTIONS

Objectives

Understanding and mastering

- why objections happen
- steps in overcoming objections
- knowing who's buying from you
- types of closes

FORM AND TECHNIQUE

Overcoming objections is a tough hill for most fitness professionals to climb. Most fitness professionals have never been in a sales atmosphere before and aren't used to people telling them *"No,"* This part of the assessment isn't really taught that much in accreditation organizations nor college curriculums. I've seen time and time again where the fitness professional will have a great workout and get to know the person very well but just isn't able to get the prospect to commit to a program. A lot of fitness professionals will allow the prospects to take over the conversation and direct the conversation to other areas to avoid this part of the assessment. Objections are basically the prospect's way of saying *not right now* or *I need more informatio*n! Usually, though, objections mask—intentionally or unintentionally—a request for more information, aka a smoke screen (little white lies that cover the truth). Becoming numb to "no" is another idea for the fitness professional to understand. All humans have a natural fear of rejection, so this is a fear that must be overcome.[52] Not everyone will commit to your program, and becoming fearful will not lead to success. Remember, the definition of closing is helping people make decisions that are good for them! Having the skill of taking every objection and interpreting it as a question for more information is a skill that is readily needed. As a fitness professional, you can leverage these objections into an opportunity to continue to build your relationship with your prospect so that you can continue to create a positive influence on the buyer's decision. The fact is, objections help you build your relationship and find the true reason for resistance. Think of objections as opportunity. Listening to the objection is a useful skill to understand and master as well. When we don't listen, we miss a lot of valuable information

Why Do Prospects Object

While prospects may voice their objections in different ways, just about every objection comes down to one of four reasons: no or not enough money, no perceived need, no sense of urgency, or no trust. John Boe, "Overcome Objections and Close the Sale," Agency Sales, September 2003, http://www.johnboe.com/articles/close_the_sale.html (accessed May 16, 2010). As the fitness professional, you have control over each one of these objections. But it's too late if you address it only when the prospect objects. In other words, you are actually handling objections at every step of the appointment.[56] Here are a few exercises to assist with mastering your craft of handling objections.

Exercises

1. Go to a local health club and go through the sales presentation as if you were going to join. What objections would you have for the salesperson? Which objections did the salesperson address to your satisfaction? Which objections did the salesperson not address to your satisfaction? Why?
2. Try to sell your professor on conducting class as a study period next week. How would you prepare for the "presentation" to make your case? What are some objections you might receive? How might you handle the objections?
3. Identify the three most common points at which objections occur in a sales presentation. Provide an example of each one in your everyday life.
4. Assume you are selling real estate, and you are calling a prospect to set up an appointment. How would you handle an objection that she doesn't have the time to meet with you?
5. Assume you are a financial services salesperson. You have presented an investment strategy to your prospect, and he has objected because he is concerned about the state of the market. How would you handle this objection by making him feel more comfortable with the risk?
6. Contact a salesperson for a local business and ask him how he handles objections. Share your findings with the class.

A Few Dos for Handling Objections[57] from "How to Identify and Overcome Objections," Edward Lowe Peerspectives.

- *Do* maintain a positive attitude and be enthusiastic.
- *Do* remember that objections are a natural part of the sales process and should not be considered as a personal affront.
- *Do* maintain good eye contact, even when under fire.

FORM AND TECHNIQUE

- *Do* listen closely to an objection.
- *Do* acknowledge the objection and then give your point of view.
- *Do* prepare to prove your position with testimonials, references, and documentation.

There are four basic objections that we are going to discuss, and we will explore how to embrace them, nurture them, and slowly resolve each of them (*money, spouse, time,* and *do it on my own*). With these steps in mind, you as a fitness professional will be able to overcome and defeat every objection that comes your way. Once you have delivered your price presentation, no matter what smoke screen the prospect raises, these are the steps to overcome the objection.

Steps in Overcoming Objections

1. *Identifying the objection: money or the sessions.* This narrows down the objection immediately to one of two things: money (affording the program or its initial cost) or the session itself (too intense, too short). Regardless of the real objection, the prospect will likely say it is the money. If they mention another objection, you want to identify it so you can understand it completely and embrace the objection. This step allows you to uncover what is truly stopping them from committing to your program.

    Fitness Professional (FP): *"Now, based on your schedule and budget, which one of these programs makes the most sense for you to get started with it today?"*
    Prospect: *"I don't know. Let me think about it ..."*
    FP: *"What would you like to think about, the money or the sessions?"*

2. *Acknowledge and repeat the objection.* Put the objection on the table and repeat what the objection is ... "So it's the money," "So it's the time," "So you have to speak with your wife," "So you want to do it on your own." This technique shows that you are listening actively and clearly understand what the prospect is saying.

FP: *"So, Mrs. Jones, it is the money that is the biggest concern. Would you agree?"*

3. *Empathize.* Empathizing is the ability to feel what the prospect feels. Let him know you feel his concern by saying, "I understand." The important central ability to feel as the prospect does in order to be able to sell him a product or service must be possessed in large measure. A seven-year field study completed by the *Harvard Business Review* stated that the basic characteristic of a successful salesperson was having empathy.[53] Having empathy doesn't necessarily mean being sympathetic. The fitness professional can know what the client feels without agreeing with that feeling. But a fitness professional simply cannot sell well without the invaluable and irreplaceable ability to get powerful feedback from the client through empathy.[53] The fitness professional can function in terms of the real interaction between himself and the customer. By sensing what the prospect is feeling, he is able to change pace, double back on his track, and make whatever creative modifications might be necessary to home in on the target and close the sale. A study published in the journal *Psychological Science*[54] suggests that ambiverts (people whose personality has a balance of extrovert and introvert features) are among the top in sales production.[54] The author of the study, Adam M. Grant, sent a personality questionnaire to outbound call center representatives. He examined the answers from the 340 employees who filled out the questionnaire in full. From the answers, the employees were assigned a level of extroversion on a scale of 1.0 to 7.0, with 1 being the highest level of introversion and 7 being the highest level of extroversion. Grant observed that while sales requires socializing and assertiveness, it also requires the salesperson to consider the "needs, interests, and values of customers."

So no matter what the objection from the prospect is, having some empathy will allow the prospect to know that you're a human too and you share feelings with them. Never argue, attack, try to prove them wrong, or compete; just show a little empathy. It's never a good idea to disagree or argue with the customer, even when he is wrong. Relationships are built on trust, so it's best to use an objection to build the trust, not break it.57 *Empathy* is always a good resolution for a fitness professional.

Car Salesman or Fitness Professional, the Story of Victor

As a fitness director over the last decade, I have seen that young fitness professionals, mainly the males, have a hard time showing empathy. Yet they are so quick to drop prices and just give themselves away. A trainer by the name of Victor was having a hard time closing deals and gaining new clientele. He was almost on the verge of quitting and throwing in the towel on his fitness career. He was big and one of my strongest trainers pound for pound. and he really knew his stuff. One day he stormed into my office and said, "I just can't do it."

I replied, "Do what?"

"They just won't buy," he responded.

So the Buddha in me told him to just sit down and take a few breaths, let his heart rate go down, and just come back to earth. Victor was tired of prospects not committing to his programs. I calmly told Victor to relax. I said, "Let's go over your entire process from start to finish, and let's look for your blind spot. Let's basically go over your game film and see what your weak tendencies are."

Victor then began to explain his sales process, and everything was good. He built rapport, he declared goals, his workout was just okay, but anyway, the blind spot finally came. It was the way he was overcoming objections! Victor would go from one set of prices to another set without any thought behind it. We role-played a few situation, and he honestly sounded like a car salesman. He would just drop prices and go for the cheapest program as soon as prospects raised any type of smoke screen. Car salesmen are masters at playing the price game. I reminded Victor, "You are not a car salesman. You are a trainer who is goal-oriented. Let's work on building some value and creating some type of empathy with the person in front of you." He was so focused on the deal that he forgot that there was a person in front of him. So for the next two weeks, we would role-play different ways of showing empathy, and he finally started to *care* for the person in front of him. Once caring became a priority, his business began to soar. He became the top trainer in my club within the next month. It was amazing. By his showing empathy and actually caring for his prospect, they sensed how much he cared. Remember, *prospects don't care how much you know until they know how much you care.*

Here are a few examples of creating empathy.

"I understand how you feel, Mrs. Jones. Most people have felt that way before, but what I've found is that if we bring our heads together, we can come up with a plan."

"I totally get it, Mrs. Jones. My wife and I talk about money all the time."

"I appreciate how you feel, Mrs. Jones. I appreciate your telling me how you feel."

4. *Building value (depending on the objection).* The fourth step after acknowledging the objection and its being brought to the table is to *build* the value back up. Usually building value is closely related to the ascending close or creating "yes momentum." These are a series of questions that usually require the answer "yes." They usually start very general and then become very specific.[52] Building value is a key component as a fitness professional because most prospects will totally forget about the workout and their goals at this point in the appointment. So you, as the results-oriented fitness professional, have to remind them of the reason why they are here again. In question form, clearly translate the features and benefits of the workout and how they are aligned with the goals set earlier.

Example Value-Building Questions

"Mrs. Jones, how did you feel from the workout?" This emphasizes workout value.

"Do you feel like workouts like this will help you to achieve your goals?" This emphasizes goals value.

"If we continued to set up scheduled appointments like the one today, your goals would be met. Do you agree?" This emphasizes accountability value.

"Do you feel like you learned a lot from today's workout?" This emphasizes knowledge value.

"Can you see how workouts like this will get you to lose 10 percent body fat?" This emphasizes goals value.

"Can you imagine how you would feel if we continued to work out like this two or three times a week?" This emphasizes goals value.

"Mrs. Jones, you did inform me earlier that you were unaware of how to put a program together, correct?" This emphasizes past history value.

"Mrs. Jones, as we talked before, you said that you have tried countless workout programs that didn't work. Would you agree?" This emphasizes previous history value.

These questions will create "*yes* momentum." The prospect should agree to most of the questions listed. Building value is a skill that should be practiced as well; deciding *where to build value is also an aim for the fitness professional based on what the prospect's objection is.* You can build value in the workout, the accountability of making the appointment, the goals that were declared earlier, past or previous fails, and the concerns that were mentioned during the price presentation. Where to aim your value building will be based solely on the prospect's objections. It will change from prospect to prospect. This is a part of mastering your craft like any great athlete; deciding where to build value will take practice and a conscious effort to choose where to build value in.

Objections to Be Overcome

Let's see how these steps can be used to answer the four categories of objections we want to discuss.

Money Objection

This is the major objection that most fitness professionals are faced with. You handle the money objection by identifying it, acknowledging, creating an environment of empathy, and then building value in the program, building value in personal goals, building value in the workout, and then creating both a *floor* and a *ceiling* budget for the prospect. Finding a new means for paying for the program might be another option as well. Finding a program that fits their budget is essential to increase your clientele and urgency, but keeping with the same step as mentioned before will feel like more of a true conversation between friends than a sale being made.

FP: *"So money is the only thing stopping us from starting a program?"*

P: *"Yes, it's not in my budget."*

FP: *"I completely understand"* (empathy). *"You are not the only one who has been in this position; I have had numerous clients who have felt the same way."*

P: *"You have?"*

FP: *"Yes, they have, but when we bring our heads together, we always come up with a plan to get the ball rolling. How did you feel from the workout?"*

P: *"Great!"*

FP: *"Do you feel like workouts like this will help us get to our goals?"*

P: *"Yes."*

FP: *"Mrs. Jones, you did agree that you weren't knowledgeable about putting together your own workout routines, correct?"*

P: *"Yes."*

FP: *"Then we agree that starting a program is necessary. We just need to find something within your budget, would you agree?"*

P: *"Yes."* (Eighty percent of the time, they will agree to the terms of finding another program that fits their budget.)

FP: *"Well, help me help you. You're the only one who knows what's going in and out of your budget. You tell me, between two hundred"* (floor) *"and five hundred"* (ceiling) *"dollars, what would you be able to budget to get a program started?"*

Once you can empathize and reestablish value in their goals, past failures, or the workout, you can find a number that they are willing to invest in starting a program. From there, as a fitness professional, be creative and find the number of sessions that caters to their budget. It may be low frequency in the beginning, but once the value is felt and results are seen, an increase in frequency will most likely be the next step.

Spouse Objection

The next objection that is most commonly received by fitness professionals is the spousal objection. *"I need to talk to my husband/wife."* It's a difficult objection because most young fitness professionals feel like it's sacred ground. The best way to deal with this objection is to take care of it before it is even brought up. During the rapport-building stage, getting to know who is *supportive* in the prospect's venture toward reaching their goals is paramount. Find out exactly if their spouse is a fitness-type person or a couch potato. Becoming their friend and developing trust will allow you to put the pieces together on whether they have the power to make financial decisions in the household or not. Keep in mind this takes practice, but from a psychological aspect, *knowing your prospect is the best way to steer clear of this objection.* This will give you some leverage when preparing to present prices. Seventy percent of the time, spousal objections are basically smoke screens, and the other thirty percent of the time, they are really holding the prospect back from starting the program. The goal is for you to be calm, breathe, and distinguish whether it is a smoke screen or a legitimate reason for not beginning. To deal with this objection, you must isolate the truth, create empathy, build value, and reclose by taking the spouse out of the picture and finding something in their individual budget or involving the spouse with the investment.

> P: *"I need to talk to my wife."*
>
> FP: *"I totally understand. You are not the only person who has been in this situation. This has happened before, and trust me, I would want my wife"* (if married) *"to talk to me as well, but just for the record, what do you want to talk to your wife about? The* money *or the* sessions?*"*
>
> P: *"The money. This program is a little out of our budget…"*
>
> FP: *"Is it more about the initial cost or the monthly investment?"* (Isolate.)
>
> P: *"The monthly investment."*
>
> FP: *"I definitely understand. We all have money issues… What do you think he will say about the price?"* (This will determine if it is a smoke screen or a true objection.)

There are two possible answers.

If it is a *smoke-screen response* , the prospect will answer, *"Umm, I think this is a little uncomfortable, but the price is too* high." Immediately show more empathy and continue with the money objection steps to overcome and find something that is in their individual budget.

Another way of looking at this scenario is to be brutally honest, first of course, by showing empathy, building value in their past failures, and then continuing to ask, "What if your wife says *no*? Then are you going to go back to your old habits of doing the same workout over and over again and never getting results?" This sets the stage for taking the spouse out of the picture and holding the prospect accountable for their own results. Then simply build value in past failures and the current situation, get them to say *"Yes,"* and create a floor and ceiling within their own budget.

If it is a true objection and the prospect says, *"I think it is perfectly fine,"* then you are dealing with a sales objection or condition. You have two choices here:

- Get the spouse involved over the phone.
- Set an appointment to come back and visit with them together. In this case, the FP can say, *"I definitely understand, and I want your spouse to have a full picture of the real value of you committing to a program. Let's bring your spouse in the next time for a short workout, and maybe you guys can start together. Let's have the both of you come in tomorrow at six o'clock. Does that work?"* Something in the nature of involving and including the spouse in the next demonstration session should align for success.

Once again, this takes a little practice, but being prepared for this objection is the best way to handle it. *Get to know your prospect as much as you can in the beginning and determine if the spouse is supportive of the prospect's goals, agrees with fitness, and is the decision maker.* This will make for a more successful commitment and appointment when tackling the spousal objection.

Time Objection

The next objection to be aware of is the time objection. *"I don't have enough time to begin a workout routine or to work with a trainer."* This is a common objection because time management is a downfall for most people to become skillful at, so they will use it as a smoke screen in order to steer away from the purchase. They have busy days at work, and then they're tired. Or they have a busy day at work, and then they forget about their workout. As humans we make time to brush our teeth, we make time to eat, and we make time to take showers. The key to the time objection is to influence the prospect to *make* time by saying *no* to other things that do not influence their health!

An article by Dr. Huff in the *Psychology Today* blog stated that "in order to be happy, what we have to do is we have to make time to be happy.

In order to do that, we have to get good at saying two specific letters of the alphabet, *N* and *O*. We have to say no to things in order to make time for overall health, and in the case for happiness, it takes time to be happy. If we don't make time to be happy, we're going to be anything but happy, and we don't want that. So part of being happy is learning to say *no* to things, and when we get overwhelmed, we just let something go.[58] The key factor here is that we have to sometimes say no to things, maybe even things that may be good for others, so in the long run, we can be good to ourselves.[58]

The best way to handle and embrace the time objection is first to identify that is the time, not the money, and acknowledge that time is the only issue holding them back. Narrow down the objection as much as you can. *"So it's time, not the money, correct? Are the workouts too long, or is it making time to actually get to the gym?"* The second step is to show empathy. *"I totally understand. I have my own issues with time, and especially after training ten people in a row, it's hard for me to want to stay here to work out. So I truly understand."* Empathize and show the prospect that they are not the only ones with time issues in regard to working out. From there, you begin to *build value* in the efficiency (the order, the organization, the quality) of the workout and how impactful the workout was in just a short matter of time or to build value in a lower frequency of times that they come to see you. Asking the client what things they can say *no* to will be an eye-opener to the array of possibilities in regard to making time. Once you have built that value with some yes momentum, offer the prospect a lower frequency program or a lower duration program. Maybe sixty minutes is too long, or maybe three times a week is too many sessions for their schedule. Start them off with a duration or frequency that they are comfortable with, and then after a few sessions, build the value in increasing the frequency or duration.

Efficiency of the Workout

"Mrs. Jones, once again, I understand time is an issue, but you felt good from the workout, correct? And everything was set up for you? You didn't have to guess what exercise to do or how to do it, correct? All of that will lead to a more efficient workout and not wasting time. These workouts are proven to make it less stressful on you and get rid of the guessing game that eighty percent

of people do when they come to the gym. Would you agree? How did you feel from the workout? Do you feel like workouts like these will help to get to your goals of better range of motion and less back stiffness? Well, let's start with thirty-minute sessions instead of sixty-minute sessions until we can get a grasp of your scheduling and time. How does that sound?"

Frequency of the Workout

"Mrs. Jones, once again, I understand time is an issue, but you felt good from the workout, correct? Based on what you told me earlier, you are unfamiliar with the gym and getting to your goals, correct? Since time is an issue, let's just shoot for one appointment a week, and we can go from there based on your schedule. One day a week will get us started and gain some knowledge in order for us to reach the goals we set. Mrs. Jones, what things can we say no *to in order for us to have time to work out?"*

We Need to Find Time ... Availability/Schedule Breakdown

"Mrs. Jones, once again, I understand time is an issue, but you felt good from the workout, correct? You would agree that if we started this program, we can get to these goals sooner rather than later? Well, Mrs. Jones, we need to make some time for change*; we need to make time for* fixing *and* healing *ourselves, wouldn't you agree? I'm available all mornings, lunches, and evenings. How do your evenings or mornings look for once a week? Mrs. Jones, what things can we say* no *to in order for us to have time to work out?"*

The time objection is a common objection that can be handled by softly *identifying, acknowledging, empathizing,* and *building value* in either the efficiency of the workout or the lower frequency of the workouts and being able to find time, along with a schedule breakdown and saying *no* to other activities. Asking for the sale again once all of the above is covered will allow for the prospect to see more opportunities to come to the gym to reach their objective. *Most prospects have blinders on, and you, the fitness professional, must take off their blinders and open their eyes to the opportunities of availability and possibilities.*

"I Can Do It on My Own" Objection

This is another common objection that most fitness professionals have to embrace and overcome. There is a lot of ego in the fitness world, especially with males. They just want to figure it out on their own. I have heard it plenty of times: *"I'll just work out with my buddy"* or *"I'll just do what you showed me, and then I can do it on my own."* The best way to handle this objection is to once again *identify, acknowledge, empathize,* and *build value* in the following areas.

1. *Concerns from Demo Workout*—imbalances, insufficient movements, postural issued, lack of mobility, lack of stability, and lack of strength, which can lead to trauma. Remember your doctor's hat!

    "Mrs. Jones, I totally understand you want to do it on your own, and you're not the only person who has felt this way, but keep in mind you have a few muscle imbalances and postural deviations that need a certain amount of attention. There are certain exercises/stretches that you must learn in order to correct some of the deviations and imbalances you have. Would you agree that your posture affects your performance?"

    Once the value of *concerns* is established, make an offer to begin a program that readily addresses the concerns. Keeping the doctor's hat on during this time will allow for a more impactful and authoritative voice.

2. *Past Failures*—looking at the prospect's past gym activities and understanding why they didn't reach their goals.

    "Mrs. Jones, I totally understand you want to do it on your own, and you're not the only person who has felt this way, but keep in mind you told me earlier that you struggle with losing weight and you have tried many times before, correct? You also shared with me that you are unfamiliar with the machines and dumbbells in the gym, is that correct? This time around, we are going to make sure you learn and educate yourself to ensure that what happened in the

past never happens again. You would agree that more education is needed, correct? And you felt good from the workout, correct?" (yes momentum)

Once the value of *past failures* is established, make an offer to begin a program that will assure that those past failures will be eradicated and they will not be an issue this time. The tone of voice should be calming and nonaggressive. Do not attack the prospect; be humble and pleasant and show that you *care*. As a fitness professional, remember people don't care how much you know until they know how much you care!

3. *The Theory of Adaptation*—If the prospect keeps performing the same workout over and over again, the body will adjust and adapt to the stressor. Changes will usually tend to cease. Emotions of frustration will usually arise once results have been diminished, and contemplation of quitting comes thereafter. A new stressor or training variable must be introduced in order for the body to resist and continual changes occur.

"Mrs. Jones, I totally understand you want to do it on your own, and you're not the only person who has felt this way, but keep in mind your first two to three months you are going to see results because this is a new stressor for your body. After the initial shock or alarm, your body will begin to adjust to the stressor, and your results will slowly halt. What causes that halt is called adaptation, *and would you agree we don't just want to stop at just five pounds when our goal is thirty-five pounds of weight loss, correct? So we are going to need to advance your workout and challenge you through altering various variables of your workout, including your sets, reps, tempo, and type of exercise you're doing. Don't you want to feel challenged every time you come in the gym? Would you agree that you want to see changes for the next six months, not just two?" Advancing your workout is going to be crucial."*

Once value is built in the *theory of adaptation* and yes momentum is created, ask for the sale again, with an emphasis on the mesocycle that was discussed in the original price presentation. Most people are very nearsighted when it comes to time to fitness goals; explaining the importance of switching the training variables will give insight into the full scope of program design and periodization and why it's impactful to deal with a fitness professional.

Know Your Buyers

The *Journal of Consumer Research* has reported there are three types of buyers: tightwads, average spenders, and spendthrifts. Tightwads and spendthrifts offer special advantages to fitness professionals.

Tightwads: Tightwads have difficulty spending money due to its relationship to pain. Leverage tightwads by reframing and reshaping the pricing of the fitness program; this will assist them in spending.

Fitness professional advantage #1: Break the session down into smaller increments; don't just show them the big price. Be creative and investigate how to utilize this in the price presentation.

Fitness professional advantage #2: Bundle, bundle, bundle. Individual purchases create different pain points, but bundles only create one. So bundle a whole bunch of your services into one set package.

Average Spenders: Once average spenders spend a little, they then will spend a lot. Average spenders are generally pretty average.

Spendthrifts: Spendthrifts have no pain point when it comes to spending money.

Fitness professional advantage: Stress the urgency of a deal. If they purchase now, they can get something free!

According to the *Journal of Consumer Research*, spending money makes some people anxious, and the problem for others is actually holding on to money.[59] The 2008 study by Rick, Cryder, and Loewenstein suggested that the "pain of spending" makes tightwads hold on to their cash.[59] To gauge how many people qualifies as spendthrifts or tightwads, Loewenstein and his colleagues surveyed more than thirteen thousand people, beginning back in 2004. Respondents reported how their scrimping and splurging diverged from their desired spending habits.

The researchers reported that 3,248 respondents proved to be tightwads, and 2,046 were spendthrifts. Percentagewise, that works out to about 25 and 16 percent of the general population, respectively.

The results also showed that males were three times more likely to be tightwads than females, who showed no bias toward either category. Spendthrifts who used credit cards, as might be expected, were three times likelier to have debt than tightwads who also swiped the plastic. Income levels did not vary much between the two camps, suggesting that spending decisions arose not from the size of one's cash pile but from ingrained spending behaviors.[59]

Types of Closes

Being able to maneuver through various ways of closing will also be a skill that will need to be practiced by the fitness professional. Every closing situation will be different and unique in its own way. Whether a prospect has a different personality or different goals that they want, as true professionals, we should be able to be agile enough to figure out a way to build value and gain commitment from our prospects. The only way closing agility can happen is by understanding some various closing styles (or a set of drills from a sports standpoint) and knowing when to put them into play. When I was a fitness director teaching closing techniques and as a trainer, learning a new way to close was like learning a new move on the basketball court. At first it was a foreign, unfamiliar movement, but after a couple of practices, it became natural and instinctive. It was another weapon added to my tool belt of weapons. Here are few closing techniques that will add value to your presentation.

Alternative Close

The alternative close works by offering more than one clearly defined alternative to the customer. The number of alternatives should be very few; two or three is often quite adequate. If you offer too many alternatives, the customer will then be faced with a more complex problem of how they choose among the many alternatives offered.[60]

Note that this technique works well in many different situations where you are seeking agreement, not just in selling products.

An extra technique that can be effective is to add a slight nod when offering the preferred choice. This can be accompanied by subtle verbal emphasis on the words.

Examples

"Would you prefer one session a week or two sessions a week?"
"Would you like one packet or two?"
"Which of these three programs seems best for you?"
"Shall we start our sessions this week or next week?"

How It Works: The alternative close is a variant on the broader-based assumptive close and works primarily through the assumption principle, where you act as if the customer has already decided to buy and the only question left is which of a limited number of options they should choose.[60]

Balance Sheet Close

This is also called the Ben Franklin close, in which the salesperson and the prospect build together a pros and cons list of whether to buy the product, with the salesperson trying to ensure the pros list is longer than the cons. This is a simple technique for the prospect to visually see the contrasts between making a commitment to a program. The fitness professional must have all the pros to commitment already listed in their head or on another sheet of paper.

Indirect Close

This is also known as the question close, in which the fitness professional moves to the close with an indirect or soft question: "How do you feel about this program" or "How does this program look to you?" These soft questions will allow the fitness professional to gauge and measure how far the prospect is from committing to a program.

Possibility of Loss Close

This is also known as the pressure close, in which the salesperson points out that failing to close could result in missed opportunity, for example, because a product may sell out or its price rise. This is a great way to increase urgency by offering a minispecial at that specific time, whether it's a free session or an opportunity to win some ancillary service. Adding incentives can be very appealing to most buyers.

"Mrs. Jones, before you came, I entered you in our system for a family incentive. Because it is your first purchase, you can receive two free massages and one free Pilates session in your package today. How does that sound?"

Puppy Dog Close

The puppy dog close is when the fitness professional gives the product to the prospect on a trial basis to test before a sale is agreed upon. This allows you to build more value and gain more trust by scheduling one or two more appointments so they can see more value in your service. This gives you another opportunity to "wow" them over with your service. It also give the fitness professional another opportunity to show how much they *care*.

Sharp Angle Close

In this close, the salesperson responds to a prospect's question with a request to close. If the prospect asks, "Can you get the system up and running within two weeks?" the salesperson can respond, "If I guarantee it, do we have a deal?"[13]

Takeaway Close

This is one of my favorites, because basically if the prospect isn't ready to make a commitment, you inform them that maybe they aren't prepared for this level of change. It's almost like you are prequalifying them, like a university not allowing a student to be admitted to their school. This takes a great deal of confidence to know that you as the fitness professional are prequalifying them for your program. The hesitation may lead to nonadherence to the program and unsuccessful results. Maybe this level of commitment isn't fitting for them at the moment.

Overcoming objections basically means being able to master various scenarios. The goal is to build up enough rapport so you can meet and address all objections *before* the prices are even shown. Practice is the key to being able to handle objections thoughtfully and skillfully. Empathy is a skill that is developed over time. People don't care how much you know until they know how much you care. Fitness professionals are in the caring business, so it's a bigger picture than just making a sale. Put forth the effort to *care* and *give*; it will make handling objections much easier and require much less effort.

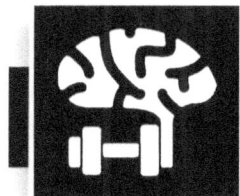

CHAPTER 6

CLIENT RENEWALS

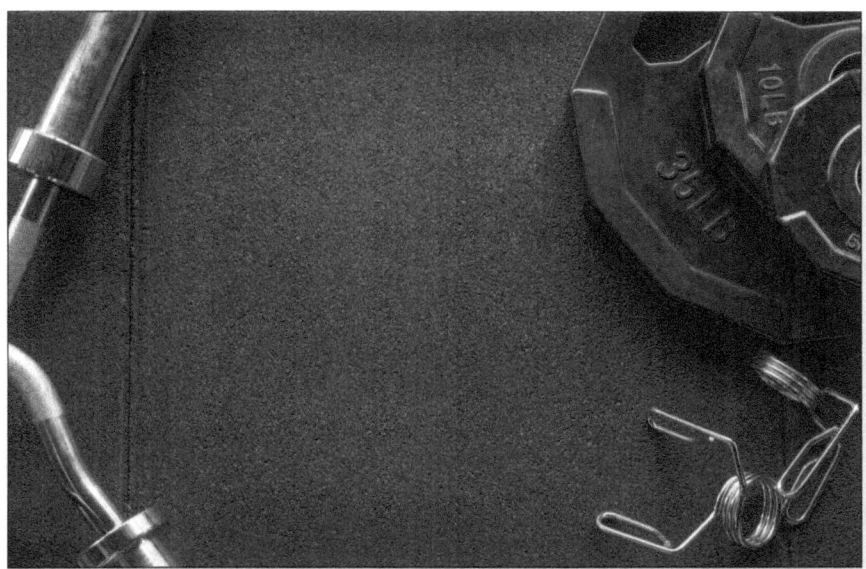

Now that you have the client's commitment, it's your responsibility to uphold your end of the bargain and get them *results*. Keep them going! Client program adherence is crucial to sustaining business and becoming a master fitness professional. Remember, we are in the business of helping and behavior change, so creating a great program is only half the issue;, we need to keep your client *renewing*!

In my early years of management, I would see trainers have clients for up to ten years! I was in awe. I couldn't believe that trainers created programs for that long a time; that's a lot of workouts! What's even more amazing was the consistency of the behavior. That's really changing lives. It really shows the relationship possibilities between trainer and client. Let's think about it. If you have been training this person for four years twice a week, I guarantee that you should know each other pretty well. You probably know about each other's families, jobs, kids, work life, and so on. The trainer-client relationship can become close. Personal training is personal!

Actually seeing clients just grab their credit cards and swipe for four thousand dollars over and over again was amazing, I wanted all my trainers to have that *power* of renewing! Imagine if I had all my trainers with such high renewal rates; I knew I would become the top fitness director in Chicago. For a period of time, I trained my trainers on client renewals and the importance of keeping clients. It's easier to resell someone than it is to sell someone new. Basically that's saying that if they bought before, they are more likely to buy again

So how can this be done? How do you get a client to keep coming back? What motivates people to keep coming back for your service?

Let's first discuss client adherence, the attachment or commitment to a person, cause, or belief. In our case, it's that commitment of a person to their workout regimen. Understanding the factors that influence a person's decision to engage in exercise behavior will be key for all fitness professionals to understand, so you can be prepared.[61] Personal attributes, environmental factors, and physical activity factors are all potential determinants that can influence adherence to exercise.

In terms of personal attributes, research says that your education, income, age, and gender can affect your adherence to exercise. The health status of an individual can have an effect on adherence; having a known disease or illness may cause the client to not work out as much. Activity history will also give you an idea of past program adherence. This is why it is so important during the initial interview to collect that data. The last personal attribute that can affect client adherence is the knowledge and attitude of the client. The perception of the client's individual health can also lead to adherence results. If your client believes and thinks they can do it, they will be more likely to continue.

Here are some more *vital* components to increase client renewals.

Always create value.

You have to demonstrate your value to your personal training clients from day one. This is no easy task. Your client's perception of your value begins at the initial intake or assessment, so make sure to make your mark right away. Use that first session to discover what that client cannot do on their own, and help them move toward that goal in a tangible way as soon as possible. Beyond that initial session, the training environment must create ongoing opportunities to add value to each client's experience.[62]

Make every interaction count.[62]

At every session, focus on the client's experience that day.

1. In the beginning of the session, ask the client, "How would you like to feel after today's training session?"
2. Identify the feeling the client stated, summarize it in a few of *their* words, and repeat it back to them to confirm.
3. Use your knowledge to tie this feeling to the client's workout for the day and their stated short-term goal.
4. Use your skills and tools (such as a trainer self-appraisal) to make workout adjustments accordingly and execute this request.
5. Check in during the session to see if the client is on track to achieve the desired outcome.
6. Make adjustments accordingly, or immediately reinforce the outcome.
7. At the end of the session ask, "Do you feel [*use the client's word or phrase from the beginning of the session*]?"
8. Address the response in a way that highlights the successful session and transfers over to the rest of their day.

The words you use matter.

Here are a few autonomy-related words/phrases that can increase enjoyment and exercise intensity.

- This should be challenging for you.
- Which exercise do you want to learn first?
- I'm curious about how you are feeling.
- These options could be combined in many ways.
- Are you willing to give it a try?
- It looks like you've mastered that exercise.
- Did you enjoy your vacation?
- Which of these exercises is most interesting to you?

Discuss the future.

Goal-setting is important, but we must also create opportunities for clients to picture themselves achieving that goal and how it will affect their lives. Use self-imagery to always place the client in a position of positivity. Help clients harness the power of imagery to cultivate intrinsic motives. Use imagery throughout a client's session, or tailor it to a client's specific needs. During preworkout stretching moves, ask clients to imagine an invigorated version of themselves, glowing in anticipation of their workout. Imagery can enhance general motivation and get clients psyched up.[63]

Elicit/evoke change talk by looking forward.

The questions below are examples of how to compare the current situation with what it would be like to not have the problem in the future (Sobell, 2008).

- "If you make changes, how would your life be different from what it is today?"
- "How would you like things to turn out for you in two years?"

Manage your customer relationships on their terms.[62]

Rarely will a client train with you because they want you to dictate exactly what to do and how to do it. Customer relationship management (CRM) has replaced customer service, which means you really need to understand what your clients want out of their sessions and work with them to achieve those goals on their terms.

Customer relationship management (CRM) *is a widely implemented model for managing a company's interactions with customers, clients, and sales prospects. The overall goals are to find, attract, and win new clients; nurture and retain those the company already has; entice former clients back into the fold; and reduce the costs of marketing and client service.*

Start your customer relationship management by finding out how your clients like to communicate. Is it text, email, or a phone call? Find out the ideal time to contact each person. Some clients appreciate a motivational quote before their morning workout or inspiration to remind them of the journey they are on. A text message (that requires no response) complimenting performance goes a long way. Other clients might want an email reminder about their next appointment, and others will simply want to be left alone.

Get social.

You may worry that if you recommend group workouts, clients will miss out on one-on-one training time or your overall fee will be lower for a group session than for the solo sessions combined. But moving clients into a social setting for workouts can be a boon to motivation. Being in a group with others who share similar goals and understand one's experiences with exercise contributes to a sense of relatedness, according to Philip M. Wilson, PhD, associate professor of kinesiology at Brock University in Saint Catharines, Ontario. That sense, in turn, has been associated with optimal motivation and well-being (Wilson & Garcia Bengoechea 2010).

Group exercise can trigger extrinsic motivations to exercise: people often feel social pressure to show up, or they may increase their level of effort to match (or outdo) other group members. Although these cues are extrinsic, they can be adaptive. Seeing others' success can help clients envision their own future achievement and adjust their own goals upward.

Be proactive with re-signing packages.

To avoid unexpected attrition, pay attention to the details of your clients' training packages. For every client, know how many hours you have trained together and how many hours remain before renewal. Start discussing future plans and renewal options with the client as early as possible. All too often, trainers err on the side of "Well, we can talk about renewing next time," only to discover that there is not a next time. Renewals are an ongoing process, not a onetime task. Be sure your every action adds value to each session, and make these actions obvious to your clients, supervisors, coworkers, and members. Know performance expectations for renewals and set personal goals based on those expectations. Open the lines of communication to your clients and communicate in a way that they find most convenient and enjoyable.

If you consistently develop these skills, you'll watch your client renewal rate increase dramatically.

Establish terms of training.

Many trainers will not allow clients to cancel more than once per twelve sessions with notice. In fact, our Pro Fitness personal training agreements have several clauses built in that we require the member to initial to ensure their commitment and success. It's not beyond some of our elite trainers to fire their clients who cancel frequently. If you're clear from the start, you're going to develop a reputation for being serious, and you will have a client base that will be getting amazing results, renewing more frequently, and referring more friends as a result of their success.

Inform prior to renewal.

At the beginning of their first session, a successful trainer should provide a road map of the phases and routines that will take a person to their goal. Regardless of how many sessions the client has committed to, the focus should still be on the bigger picture. With three to five sessions remaining prior to the renewal, a trainer should be handing the client information on the next phase of the program that outlines what the client can expect in terms of routines and results. This will give them time to take the information home, digest it, and start imagining what the next step will look like in terms of goals and results. They will be far better prepared to accept your renewal offer when the time comes.

Add variety.

Spice it up! If you have been doing mobility stretches and core movements for two months, switch it up to HIIT for a brief moment. If you remember the story of Dionte Russell, he was all barbells and dumbbells when I first hired him as a trainer. He was having trouble renewing clients, but then he suffered an injury, gained two more specialty certifications, and literally reinvented himself. He had more weapons in his arsenal that he could bring to his client. Dionte never had an issue renewing after that.

Dionte was able to spice up his sessions with new modalities, new stretches, and concepts that he added. That added knowledge and fine-tuning created more value in his sessions. Whether it's flexibility, Pilates, yoga, endurance, sports specific, balance, plyos, power training, or core training, keep things fresh and exciting. All workouts should be exciting and an experience.

Ask for testimonials and referrals.[64]

Do you avoid asking for client endorsements because you don't want to seem too intrusive or pushy? If so, you may be missing out on a motivational tool (not to mention a marketing advantage). Saying good things about a club, trainer, or program may enhance a client's motivation to continue the relationship, since it is a link between commitment and consistency (or adherence).

"Once a stand is taken, there is a natural tendency to behave in ways that are stubbornly consistent with that stand," according to social influence expert Robert Cialdini, PhD, professor emeritus of psychology and marketing at Arizona State University (Cialdini 2007). People often infer their own attitudes from their behavior, so clients who make positive statements about a fitness or wellness professional may be convinced by their own comments—and become increasingly committed to the partnership.

Don't be afraid to ask clients for endorsements. Research by Polish psychologists shows that requests made in the context of casual conversation are most likely to be effective (Dolinski, Nawrat & Rudak 2001). Mention your new website or upcoming boot camp, and then ask if your client would be willing to write a brief statement of what he's gained from working with you. Giving testimonials reminds clients of the benefits they get from exercise so they want to keep doing it.

Make 'em feel good.

This is probably the most important tool that I have used in my management, teaching, and fitness career. Make clients feel good when the session is complete. I have taught this to over three hundred trainers in my career, and they all have benefited from this piece of advice. When people leave a massage, they leave feeling a sense of accomplishment and the feeling of endorphins secreted through the body. That truly feels good!

Why can't we give our clients the same feeling? I'm not saying to go get a massage license, but I am saying learn some manual stretch modalities that make people feel good! End the session ten to fifteen minutes early and invest the time to help them gain the equilibrium and energy to do whatever once the session is complete by giving them a well-rounded cooldown. This is vital to making the client feel relaxed and a feeling of accomplishment. Having them release all the tension that was built up from the workout session will feel like a weight being lifted off them. They will go into the locker room feeling light and wanting to come back.

All in all, your clients are your universe, and people don't care how much you know until they know how much you care! Take everything they say seriously and with some accountability. Really, really *listen*; they are giving you clues about them as a person and their attitudes and behaviors, so pay attention. Your service and the way you treat your client will separate you from the rest.

The skills, traits, secrets, and research collected in this book should give every fitness professional a base for development. Keep in mind it is just a base ... you will have to build on the base of this book by constantly being mindful of every interaction, set, rep, movement, and behavior of your own and those of your client. Practicing the skills and techniques explained in this book is the *only* way to become successful. Not every technique in this book may be for you or matches your style, but just having the awareness of the technique makes you *stronger* and more *knowledgeable*.

The fitness professional who practices the techniques outlined in this book will be more confident, efficient, and sharp at their profession. Deep practice is the key to success. Take every moment and learn from it. Deliberately try to improve your technique; perfect your weaknesses.[66] Get better! It will make the sale easier, cause you less anxiety, and get you more swag! It's okay to make a mistake because it will make you smarter.

The answer is neurological. Myelin is a neural substance that wraps around and insulates the fibers of your nerve cells like beads on a string, improving the speed and accuracy with which bioelectrical signals (in other words, thoughts) travel through the brain.[66] The ability to have confidence and increase client loyalty are the fruits of practicing and mastering your craft.

Desire to be the best! That is the key to mastering your craft and unlocking your potential. As a fitness director, I want my team to have the most sessions completed and the most revenue coming in Chicago! That is what ignited me to want to be the best. Also, being the highest paid fitness director was a low-hanging fruit that motivated me. According to Dan Coyle, deep practice cannot exist without an ignition, so find your *motivation*!

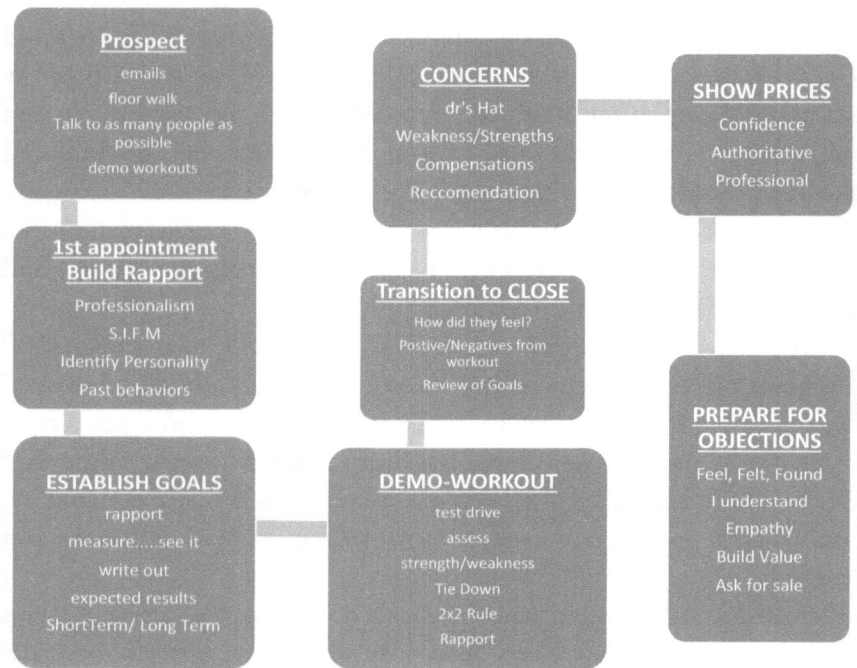

The Flow Chart is a resource to use to ensure that all aspects of sales technique are being applied.

DO NOT miss any steps on flow chart.

Master all steps on flow chart to increase clientele, and closing percentage.

If this flow chart is mastered and every step is followed closing % will increase and more value will be added to every PT assessment appointment!

Practice like you've never WON, and PERFORM like you never LOST!

ACKNOWLEDGMENTS

I would like to thank all the managers and coworkers who have influenced me and given me the guidance I needed over the last twelve years. All of the manager meetings, individual meetings, conference calls, late nights in the gym, and power points finally have done some good. I would also like to thank all the trainers whom I have hired over the last twelve years and who have listened to me ramble and ramble about the psychology of pt sales. I would also like to say thank you to all my exercise science students at Malcolm X College and Benedictine University for giving me feedback and ideas about the book. Finally, I would like to thank my mother, Eunice Magnus, and my beautiful wife, Timeesha Magnus, who has always been there to support me.

Greatness is a lot of small things done well.

BIBLIOGRAPHY

1   Winning the Retention Battle: Fitness Industry Association, 2001. *reviewing key issues of UK health & fitness club membership retention.*
2   2016 IHRSA Profile of Success Industrial Data Survey. *November 2, 2016* in IHRSA.
3   Brooks bush Institute. Human Movement Sciences Panel Discussion: Trainer Attrition: What's wrong? Brentbrookbush.com.
4   www.influencepeople.biz. February 16, 2015 Brian Ahearn, CMCT.
5   Cialdini's principle of Persuasion. Influence Science Practices.
6   Social influence. The Ontario Symposium Vol 5.
7   Suedfield, Bochner, Mates 1971. Journal of Applied Social Psychology Petitioner's Attire and Petition Signing by Peace Demonstrators: A Field Experiment[1].
8   Drachman, Decarufel, Insko 1978. Exploring The efficacy of Compliments. Journal **Basic and Applied Social Psychology** Volume 32, 2010-Issue 3.
9   Aronson, Turner, Carlsmith 1963. The Theory of Cognitive Dissonance: A Current Perspective. Advances in Experimental Social Psychology Volume 4, 1969, Pages 1–34.
10 Aronson, Turner, Carlsmith 1963. EFFECT OF THE SEVERITY OF THREAT ON THE DEVALUATION OF FORBIDDEN BEHAVIOR 1 ELLIOT ARONSON University of Minnesota J. MERRILL CARLSMITH2 Harvard University.
11 Worchel, S., Lee, J., & Adewole, A. (1975). Effects of supply and demand on ratings of object value. *Journal of Personality and Social Psychology, 32*(5), 906–914.
12 ACE PT Manual 5th Edition.
13 McCrae, R. R. and Costa P. T. (1987) Validation of the Five Factor Model of Personality across Instruments and Observers. Journal of Personality and Social Psychology, 52, 81–90.
14 FMS: North American Journal of Sports and Physical Therapy. 2010 June 5 (2) 47–54.
15 www.acefiness.org/blog/5413/.
16 Blog.hubspot.com/marketing/business.

17 *Sport Psychology for Youth Coaches: Developing Champions in Sports and Life* Frank Smoll, Ph.D.
18 University of Southern California. "Making a mistake can be rewarding, study finds: MRI study shows failure is a rewarding experience when the brain has a chance to learn from its mistakes." ScienceDaily. ScienceDaily, 25 August 2015. <www.sciencedaily.com/releases/2015/08/150825103111.htm>.
19 Consumer Behavior www.helpscout.net:Full Cycle Social Psychology, Action Paralysis.
20 Leventhal, H., Singer, R., & Jones, S. (1965). Effects of fear and specificity of recommendation upon attitudes and behavior. *Journal of Personality and Social Psychology, 2*(1), 20-29. *Send to*
21 McLean, Sionnadh Mairi, et al. "Appointment reminder systems are effective but not optimal: results of a systematic review and evidence synthesis employing realist principles." *Patient preference and adherence* 10 (2016): 479.
22 Christensen, Aaron A., R. A. Lugo, and D. K. Yamashiro. "The effect of confirmation calls on appointment-keeping behavior of patients in a children's hospital dental clinic." *Pediatr Dent*23.6 (2001): 495–498.
23 Woculus.com: How to confirm appts.
24 www.prochange.com/transthoretical model of behavior change.
25 Changingminds.org.
26 Carnegie Melon University-nuroeconomicshttps://www.helpscout.com/blog/cheap-customers/.
27 www.forbes.com: "How to Tell a Good Story."
28 Consumer Behavior: 10 Psychology Studies on Marketing and …
29 https://www.helpscout.com/consumer-behavior/ "embrace the power of internal labels."
30 www.helpscout.com: Immediate gratification.

   a. The economics of immediate gratification. Ted O'Donoghue Matthew Mabin29 March 2000. Journal of Behavioral Decision Making.
   b. Kingston, K M. and Hardy, L. *Effects of different types of goals upon processes that support performance* The Sport Psychologist (in press).

[Google Scholar]

   c. Kingston, K. M. and Hardy, L. *Situational specificity in goal orientations amongst golfers of differing ability levels* (in preparation).

31 Kingston, K., Hardy, L. and Markland, D. 1992. A study to compare the effect of two different goal orientations and stress levels on a number of situationally relevant performance sub-components. *Journal of Sports Sciences*, 47: 610–611.
32 Weinberg, R. and Butt, J. 2005. "Goal-setting in sport and exercise domains: The theory and practice of effective goal-setting". In *Handbook of research in applied sport psychology*, Edited by: Hackfort, D., Duda, J. and Lidor, R. 129–146. Morgantown, WV: Fitness Information Technology.
33 Weinberg, R., Burton, D., Yukelson, D. and Weigand, D. 1993. Goal-setting in competitive sport: An exploratory investigation of practices of collegiate athletes. *The Sport Psychologist*, 7: 275–289.
34 Gill, Diane, Lavon Williams, and Erin Reifsteck. Psychological dynamics of sport and exercise. Human Kinetics, 2017.
35 Bandura, Albert. "Self-efficacy: toward a unifying theory of behavioral change." *Psychological review* 84.2 (1977): 191.
36 Callow, Nichola, and Lew Hardy. "Types of imagery associated with sport confidence in netball players of varying skill levels." *Journal of applied sport psychology* 13.1 (2001): 1–17.
37 Martin, Kathleen A., Sandra E. Moritz, and Craig R. Hall. "Imagery use in sport: A literature review and applied model." *The sport psychologist* 13.3 (1999): 245–268.
38 www.collegsportscholarship.com/manualresistancetraining.
39 Psychology Today. Health Professional.com Ryan Howes.
40 Kiesler, Sara, and Jonathon N. Cummings. "What do we know about proximity and distance in work groups? A legacy of research." *Distributed work* 1 (2002): 57–80.
41 Blass, Thomas. "Understanding behavior in the Milgram obedience experiment: The role of personality, situations, and their interactions." *Journal of personality and social psychology* 60.3 (1991): 398.
42 www.amtamassage.org/effectivepalpations.
43 Gazzaniga, Michael S., R. B. Ivry, and G. R. Mangun. "Cognitive Neuroscience, New York: W. W." (2002).
44 Wegner, Daniel M., et al. "Paradoxical effects of thought suppression." *Journal of personality and social psychology* 53.1 (1987): 5.
45 Blankenship, Kevin L., and Traci Y. Craig. "Language and persuasion: Tag questions as powerless speech or as interpreted in context." *Journal of Experimental Social Psychology* 43.1 (2007): 112–118.
46 Hoffelsgroup.com/psychology/what is yourclient thinking about.
47 Dr. Christian Jarret: The British Psychological Society Research Digest Blog.
48 www.mindtools.com/buildingrapport.

49 Tamir, Diana I., and Jason P. Mitchell. "Disclosing information about the self is intrinsically rewarding." *Proceedings of the National Academy of Sciences* 109.21 (2012): 8038–8043.
50 National Bureau of Economic Research https://www.nber.org/
51 https://soapboxhq.com/blog/employee-motivation/help-employees-take-ownership-work.
52 Brain Tracey: The Psychology of Sales www.briantracy.com.
53 Harvard Business review: What makes a good salesman?
54 Grant, Adam M. "Rethinking the extraverted sales ideal: The ambivert advantage." Psychological Science 24.6 (2013): 1024–1030.
55 https://www.zs.com/-/media/files/publications/private/whitepapers/value-based-selling-achieving-sales-success-in-the-medical-device-equipment-and-diagnostics-industry.pdf.
56 The Power of Selling; saylordotorg.github.
57 How to Overcome Patient Recruitment Roadblocks-NC TraCS … https://propertibazar.com/ … /how-to-overcome-patient-recruitment-roadblocks-nc-trac … How to Identify and Overcome Objections-Bank SETA. Aug 11, 2004-Edward Lowe. … Identify and Overcome. Objections. An Edward Lowe In-Depth Business.
58 Robert Puff Ph.D. | Psychology Today. https://www.psychologytoday.com/us/experts/robert-puff-phd Robert Puff Ph.D. Dr. Robert Puff is an internationally recognized Speaker and Clinical Psychologist who helps companies and … Meditation for Modern Life.
59 Rick, Scott I., Cynthia E. Cryder, and George Loewenstein. "Tightwads and spendthrifts." *Journal of Consumer Research* 34.6 (2007): 767–782.
60 Changingminds.org.
61 Dishman, Rod K., and Janet Buckworth. *Adherence to physical activity*. Taylor & Francis, 1997. 4 Make-or-Break Client Renewal Tips for Trainers | Article | PTontheNet www.ptonthenet.com/articles/4-make-or-break-client-renewal-tips-for-trainers-3629.
62 4 Make-or-Break Client Renewal Tips for Trainers | Article | PTontheNet www.ptonthenet.com/articles/4-make-or-break-client-renewal-tips-for-trainers-3629.
63 Munroe, Krista J., et al. "The four Ws of imagery use: Where, when, why, and what." *The Sport Psychologist* 14.2 (2000): 119–137.
64 www.ideafit.com/ 6ways for client renewal.
65 Schultz, P. Wesley, et al. "The constructive, destructive, and reconstructive power of social norms." *Psychological science* 18.5 (2007): 429–434.
66 Coyle, D. (2009). *The Talent code: Greatness isn't born, it's grown*. First edition. New York: Bantam Books.

www.ingramcontent.com/pod-product-compliance
Lightning Source LLC
Chambersburg PA
CBHW020434220526
45464CB00002B/694